OUT FROM
LAS
VEGAS

ADVENTURES A DAY AWAY

FLORINE LAWLOR
WITH ANDY ZDON

SPOTTED
DOG PRESS

D1160940

OUT FROM
LAS
VEGAS

ADVENTURES A DAY AWAY

FLORINE LAWLOR
WITH ANDY ZDON

**SPOTTED
DOG PRESS.**

OUT FROM LAS VEGAS
ADVENTURES A DAY AWAY

©1989-2007 Florine Lawlor
All rights reserved. Published exclusively by Spotted Dog Press, Inc.
Spotted Dog Press is a registered trademark of Spotted Dog Press, Inc.

www. SpottedDogPress.com

We welcome your comments and ideas. Please write us at:
Spotted Dog Press, Inc.
P.O. Box 1721
Bishop, CA 93515-1721
or email us: wbenti@spotteddogpress.com
Call TOLL FREE to order: 800-417-2790 FAX: 760-872-1319

New text updates, Desert Travel ©2002-2007 Andy Zdon
Cathedral Gorge & Bullionville, The Extra Terrestrial Highway, Desert Travel ©2002-2007 Wynne Benti
Maps ©1998-2007 Spotted Dog Press, Inc.

Second edition, fourth printing (updated 2007)
ISBN 1-893343-07-3
All photos by the author unless noted otherwise.
Cover: Sunset over the Basin and Range. Photo: Andy Zdon
Cover Inset: Russ White at Valley of Fire State Park. Photo: Andy Zdon
Back Cover Insets: Petroglyphs; Nevada desert wash. Photos: Leslie Payne
Back Cover: The Extra Terrestrial Highway. Photo: Wynne Benti

Library of Congress Cataloging-in-Publication Data
Lawlor, Florine.
        Out From Las Vegas: adventures a day away / Florine Lawlor with Andy Zdon.
        p. cm.
        Includes index.
        ISBN 1-893343-07-3
        1. Las Vegas Region (Nev.) Tours. 2. Automobile Travel -- Nevada
        Las Vegas Region Guidebooks . I. Zdon, Andy, 1960- II. Title.
        F849.L35 L388 2002
        917.93' 1350434 — dc21   2002067039

Printed in the United States of America

A WORD ABOUT SAFETY

Certain risks and hazards are associated with traveling in the remote desert and mountain regions of Nevada. Some of these hazards include, but are not limited to: vehicle breakdown many miles from services; range cattle, wildlife, motorcycles or ATVs on or crossing roadways; adverse weather conditions, unpredictable flash floods, stream crossings, sand drifts, loose rock and rockfall, rugged terrain, potential for insect, snake or animal bites, hypothermia, heat stroke and heat exhaustion, hyponatremia, and dehydration.

Roads may wash out due to flash flooding or be impassable due to drifting sand or unexpected snow. Road crews may not have signs up which notify of closures on maintained roads, and don't expect to see signs warning of closures on unmaintained roads.

Make sure your vehicle is in good running condition with at least one good spare tire, a basic tool kit, and carry a good map knowing how to read it. **Recommended maps:** Benchmark Maps Road & Recreation Atlas series; the Automobile Association of America (AAA) road maps. Check individual USGS topographic maps for more detailed information. Always check ahead with the managing land agency for pertinent information, as conditions are constantly changing. Please read the section on desert travel in the back of this book.

Carry plenty of water, extra food, blankets or sleeping bags, and warm clothing. Let someone know your travel plans, where you are going, when you plan to return, even if you have a cell phone. There are still many areas without cell phone service.

Though all routes were scouted, the author and publisher of this guide make no representations as to the safety of any route described in this book. There is no substitute for common sense when traveling and exploring the backroads and mining country of Nevada.

A WORD ABOUT ARCHAEOLOGICAL SITES AND ARTIFACTS

Archaeological sites and artifacts are protected by the Antiquities Act of 1906 and the Archaeological Resources Protection Act of 1979. All historic and prehistoric sites on federal lands are protected and defacement, removal, excavation or destruction of such antiquities is prohibited by law.

ABOUT THE AUTHOR

Florine looks out on Mt. Charleston. Photo by Leslie Payne

Las Vegas native Florine Lawlor was born to write about Nevada's backroads. Granddaughter of a Nevada railroad man, her father once worked the gold mines at the now abandoned mining camp of Delamar. If there is a story known about the history of Las Vegas or Nevada, Florine is the one to tell it. According to Ms. Lawlor, "While I love to write and research, I prefer exploring Nevada to anything else in the world." She has been an entrusted confidant to the old-timers, the miners, and tribal elders, listening to their stories and in turn retelling them in her wonderful style.

Her Las Vegas column "Adventures A Day Away" established her as an expert on the backroads and history of her beloved Nevada, while her articles and stories have been published in several magazines including: *Arizona Highways, Desert Magazine, Las Vegas Magazine, National Parks Magazine, Nevada Magazine, Prime Magazine, Sierra Magazine, Sunset Magazine, Southwest Art, Treasure,* and *the Los Angeles Times Travel Section.*

Joining Ms. Lawlor on this new edition, is Andy Zdon, author of *Desert Summits: A Climbing & Hiking Guide to California and Southern Nevada.* A geologist, Mr. Zdon lived in Las Vegas and Central Nevada for many years and authored the American Institute of Professional Geologists handbook, *Geology of the Las Vegas Region,* before moving to the Eastern Sierra Nevada.

CONTENTS

FOREWORD

People from all over the world travel to Las Vegas to enjoy the exquisite hotels, fabulous casinos, crowded lounges, gourmet restaurants, and all-you-can eat buffets which are open twenty-four glittering hours a day. While the city's halo of lights illuminates the sky, just outside its perimeter, Nevada's backroads are ready and waiting to be explored.

While the desert air whispers forgotten stories of old mining men who once told of hillsides covered with gold and lost mines hidden in distant ranges, Nevada's backroads will take you there. Distant horizons call to you just as they called to ancient people who were the first to make the trails. The lost mines and ghost towns are still there. Gold, silver, turquoise, and other treasures can still be found in the hills and canyons, but to do so takes time, patience, and diligent searching.

The trips I've included in this book are as accurate as I could make them. However, roads come and go in the desert, changing with each rain and windstorm. Directions to lost mines are vague, while rockslides and earthquakes change even the mighty mountains. Streams and springs dry up and reappear in other locations. Drifting sand conceals lost treasure and roads. The only sure thing about the Nevada desert is change itself.

For all of you who venture forth on these trips to Nevada's beautiful desert backcountry, I hope you find them as exciting and fascinating as I have.

Florine Lawlor
Las Vegas, Nevada

A WORD FROM THE PUBLISHER

Nevada is the last great desert frontier in the contiguous United States. North of Las Vegas, above the sage-covered desert, where the skies are hazy blue, the Great Basin's range country is defined by alpine environments where aspens and pines shade the traces of last winter's snow on northern slopes. In contrast, Nevada's basins are decorated by colorful mesas, orange cottonwood leaves in autumn, and herds of wild horses and burros. Those who view Nevada as a vast desolate wasteland are very wrong—it is simply an incredibly beautiful place.

We would like to thank the rangers at the Las Vegas BLM Field Office and Red Rock National Conservation Area for taking the time to review this book and provide their written comments to us. We thank our readers who sent us their field notes regarding inaccessibility to areas due to new construction and private property closures, damage to areas from vandalism, littering, and "rogue" off-road vehicle use. Several trips in the first edition have been removed because they no longer exist, gone forever–replaced by new streets and neighborhoods. Located in what was once Nevada's largest Anasazi settlement, the thousand year-old Mesa House, described in the first edition, was turned to dust by ATVs. Readers of this edition are directed to a reconstruction of Mesa House at the Lost City Museum in Overton.

Andy Zdon, author of *Desert Summits: A Climbing & Hiking Guide to California and Southern Nevada* and the American Institute of Professional Geologists handbook, *Geology of the Las Vegas Region*, rescouted routes and worked with various park agencies to update the information in this edition.

Wynne Benti, Spotted Dog Press, Inc.

NORTH
OF LAS VEGAS

SHEEP MOUNTAINS AND MORMON WELL

The Sheep Mountains do not boast of towering peaks or magnificent heights. Some of the most ruggedly spectacular scenery in southern Nevada lies within their domain. Patronage by man has so far taken little toll, for roads leading in and out of the mountains are rough and seldom traveled. In the furthest reaches are narrow, sage-strewn meadows broken occasionally by tumbled outcrops and vast stretches of verdant forests. An ancient trail leading over the mountains was used by nomadic Indians and early settlers traveling from Las Vegas to Pahranagat Valley.

Corn Creek, at the foot of the Sheep Mountains, was a natural camping ground for those on their way to and from Pahranagat Valley by way of the Mormon Well Trail. Seed grasses and other edible plants in the sand dune area provided food for animals. Abundant water drew game from miles around.

Near all the springs in the Corn Creek vicinity are relics of early mans visits. In the foothills of the Sheep Mountains a few hundred feet above the dunes is a network of trails. Some lead to nothing while others take you past sagging shacks and piles of rusted cans left by some long-forgotten fortune seeker.

There are two trails passing over the mountains from Corn Creek. One trail wanders into Pahranagat Valley via White Sage Flat, Cone Mountain, through Cabin Springs Dry Lake and Owl Valley. The other trail passes by Fossil Ridge, Rainbow Mountain, Cave Hill, and over Mormon Well Pass. It continues to the Alamo-Pahranagat Valley Road several miles from the small town of Alamo. Visitors planning to tour either area are asked to stop at the

THE SHEEP MOUNTAINS
DESERT NATIONAL WILDLIFE RANGE

The Desert National Wildlife Range encompasses over 1.5 million acres of diverse desert shrub and coniferous forest habitat for the desert bighorn sheep and many other species.

To Alamo and Pahranagat

EAST DESERT RANGE

SHEEP RANGE

SAWMILL SPRING

HAYFORD PEAK

Wire Grass Spring (cabin site)

HIDDEN FOREST

Alamo Road (old road to Alamo)

Mormon Well Road

MORMON WELL

Historical Mormon Well was first recorded in 1896 and has since served as a watering hole for travelers and livestock. The old corral on the north side is listed in the National Register of Historical Places.

Carrying, possessing or discharging firearms, or other explosives including fireworks, inside the refuge is strictly prohibited.

LAS VEGAS RANGE

Agave Roasting Pit

Sheep Mountain Range Bighorn Habitat

CORN CREEK FIELD STATION

HWY 95

TO LAS VEGAS

N
W   E
S

©2007 SDP, Inc. Map not to scale

Forest at Mormon Well

Corn Creek Ranger Station and register. Overnight camping is allowed along either route, as long as one camps within a hundred feet of the roads, and does not drive off the road. However, for non-campers, each route is short enough to allow plenty of time for day-time exploring. Because camping regulations can change, it is recommended that the Desert National Wildlife Refuge is contacted before heading out with the tent in tow.

Six miles south of Mormon Well Road, the red and orange sandy slates common throughout the Sheep Mountains come into view. These particular outcrops contain fossils and fragments of white quartzite dating back millions of years to the Devonian Period. Ridges extend for a thousand feet or more. Many fossils can be found every step of the way.

Thick forests clothe the rolling hillsides in green. Among the trees, where erosion has exposed the rocks, an untold variety of Nature's uniquely shaped sculptures are found. In spots the crests of the higher hills are shaped like great fortresses. A large erosion hole looks much like the watchful eye of Argus. The nomadic Indians believed these spirit eyes to be special places where the Great Spirit could be seen, and that he watched over them through this opening. Nearby is the twisted form of an ancient Bristlecone pine.

Nearing Mormon Well Pass, one becomes aware of the many trails that lead over the wooded hills. Ancient people left flakes of chert and pottery fragments, subtle reminders of their presence.

A land unscathed by human destruction is found at the very doorway of Las Vegas. Hopefully, the Sheep Mountains will stay this way for years to come. They are threatened daily by encroachment from ever expanding Las Vegas suburbs. Sometime in the near future, visit the Sheep Mountains. Take the Alamo Road or the Mormon Well Road. Park your car and explore the forest, the rocks, springs and dry lake, but most of all explore the ancient trails leading to ultima Thule.*

Editors note: for those who thought that ultima Thule was located in Nevada (and have spent hours trying to find it on a map) it's not, at least not literally. It can be found in The American Heritage Dictionary of the English Language: ultima Thule: 1. The northernmost region of the habitable world as thought of by ancient geographers. 2. A remote goal or ideal [Latin].

DIRECTIONS

From Las Vegas, take Highway 95 north approximately 23 miles to the signed exit "Desert National Wildlife Refuge" at Corn Creek Station Road. Exit and turn right on the dirt road. Just past Corn Creek Station (about four miles from Highway 95), the road divides. The right fork goes to Mormon Well in the Sheep Mountains, about 28 miles. Two-wheel drive vehicles with high clearance are recommended although most any car can reach Corn Creek Station, a pleasant stop worthy in its own right of a visit.

The Desert National Wildlife Refuge, one of the country's oldest wildlife refuges, was established in 1936 to protect the bighorn sheep that reside here. Camping is permitted within 100 feet of any road (without driving off-road) in the refuge. Do not camp within one quarter mile of any spring. Not only is it against Refuge regulations, but human activity disrupts the wildlife that makes the area their home. Contact the Desert National Wildlife Refuge office in Las Vegas for more information on the Sheep Mountains.

Recommended basic maps: AAA Nevada/Utah road map; Benchmark Maps Nevada Road & Recreation Atlas. Check individual topographic maps for more detailed information.

HIDDEN FOREST

Hidden Forest has played a relatively small role in the history of southern Nevada, no doubt due to its obscure location. Early pioneers attempting to call it home faced incredible difficulties. Mormons tried to settle the area and operate a sawmill on the eastern slope of the Sheep Range. Timber was found in abundance, yet no water supply could be located, a condition that would have discouraged any but the most hardy breed of trailblazer. They built the mill with the object of running it only during the winter months when snow could be melted to furnish water for the boilers. The venture proved to be unprofitable and was abandoned after a short time.

Unknown, save to a few prospectors and Mormon settlers, this remarkable forest might have remained terra incognita had it not been for Governor James G. Scrugham. He organized an expedition and set out to learn its secrets. His party included scientists who could study and classify the forest flora and fauna. A tractor and a scraper were utilized to break a road that would permit passage of a car through brush and rocks.

The party was successful in motoring to the forest with little difficulty. The findings were described by Scrugham as follows:

One of the most interesting features of the place is its great variety of trees. During the short visit of the exploring party in the forest, six species of conifers and many small shrubs were identified. The conifers include the pinyon and juniper trees of the lower altitudes and the yellow pine, foxtail pine, Pinus albicaulis, and white fir of the higher altitudes. Of the latter group, the foxtail pine is the most interesting. It is seen in dense groves

Florine's husband, Jim, in the Hidden Forest

with its long thin branches draped from all angles, much resembling fox-tails. The foxtail pine is an uncommon evergreen and this grove is the only one ever reported to exist in the state. Among the shrubs are several varieties of mountain mahogany, buckbrush and many unidentified low bushes. Around the springs are a variety of marsh grasses, willows, quaking aspen and alder. In the lower part of the canyon there is a veritable wilderness of desert growth which includes cholla and barrel cactus, prickly pear and yucca palm.

Mountain sheep are the most numerous large animals on half the range and there obviously exist many predatory animals such as wildcats and mountain lions. The sheep remain on the mountain during summer months and with the coming of the snows descend to the warmer foothills. There are but a few small animals, the only ones seen being chipmunks and pack rats. Birds are also a rarity, though a greater variety may appear during summer. The only ones noticed were the Clarks crow, the junco, and a species of small woodpecker.

In prehistoric times a frequently traveled Indian trail extended from the Charleston Mountains to the Colorado River. This trail passed directly through the Hidden Forest, where many of the ancients made their homes. That the old tribes lived in the forest has been definitely established by the finding of pottery fragments and the presence of many old fire pits where the root of the mescal plant was roasted to be eaten for food or brewed into liquor. A deeply worn trail was found which leads to a supposed temple of sun worship. This temple consists of a series of concentric rings in the lava formation on the side of a hill, with a central altar of stone supposed to have been used for sacrificial purposes. The temple stones were laid long ago and are glossy with the patina of great antiquity. The history of the people who lived in the Hidden Forest long ago may never be known.

Only the fragments of pottery and the dimly marked circles of heaped stones record their passing. Hidden Forest remains, with its venerable trees and shading boughs, to rest and interest the desert traveler, and is one of the most remarkable scenic attractions of our state.

*Editor Andy Zdon enjoys the tranquility on the summit of Hayford Peak, 9,912',
highpoint of the Sheep Range, located inside the Desert National Wildlife Refuge. Established by
Congress in 1936 as a sanctuary for the bighorn sheep, the refuge encompasses an area of 2,200
square miles, making it the largest wildlife refuge of its kind in the contiguous United States.
The summit of Hayford was reached via Deadman Canyon. Photo: Wynne Benti*

The wayfarer, who essays the passage of mile upon mile of wilderness, turns his car toward that apparently sterile range, and emerges through the towering gorge into the heart of the forest will have more than just an excursion into a scene of transcendental beauty. He will have an emotional adventure, for the long journey through the wasteland terminating with the dramatic entry into Hidden Forest, is almost like an allegory of a passage from the valley of tribulation to the hills of paradise.

DIRECTIONS

From Las Vegas, take Highway 95 north approximately 23 miles to the signed exit "Desert National Wildlife Refuge" at Corn Creek Station Road. Turn right (east) and follow a well-graded dirt road 4. 1 miles to the signed Alamo/Mormon Well Road junction just past the Corn Creek Ranger Station (where there is a nice little museum, flora display and a guest register book). Turn left and head north 8.8 miles to the signed Cow Camp Road. Stay left and continue 6.2 miles to the signed Hidden Forest Road. Drive 3.6 miles east to the road end at a locked gate, the mouth of Deadman Canyon and the trailhead for Hidden Forest.

The graded dirt roads are in good to fair condition and two-wheel drive vehicles should have no problem getting to the Hidden Forest trailhead. From the trailhead, the old dirt road can be hiked five miles one way to an old cabin at Wiregrass Spring. Camping is permitted within 100 feet of any road (without driving off-road) in the refuge. Do not camp within one quarter mile of any spring. Not only is it against Refuge regulations, but human activity disrupts the wildlife that makes the area their home. Backcountry camping is permitted at the Hidden Canyon cabin. Further information on the Sheep Mountains can be obtained by contacting the Desert National Wildlife Refuge office in Las Vegas.

Recommended basic maps: AAA Nevada/Utah road map; Benchmark Maps Nevada Road & Recreation Atlas. Check individual topographic maps for more detailed information.

THE OLD ROAD TO ALAMO

A paradoxical land lies between the mighty Colorado River and the Spring Mountains of Southern Nevada. Sage, creosote, and mesquite are only a few of the native plants that add a shade of green or silver to the sandy landscape. Like islands in a sea of gray desolation, these oases are utterly incongruous to their surroundings. It is here that flora and fauna flourish in a bewildering variety and luxuriant abundance. Several such beautiful and unspoiled paradises exist on the "Old Road to Alamo."

The traveler, who speeds by the Desert National Wildlife Refuge sign on Highway 95, will pass not far from the strange Hidden Forest. Unless he has obtained specific information regarding its whereabouts, he will continue his journey unaware that such a fascinating place is so close to Las Vegas.

At the Corn Creek Station, Desert National Wildlife Refuge sign, a dirt road leaves the main highway and heads eastward toward a high rampart of desert mountains. At first glance, the mountains appear utterly barren and without life. Situated as it is at the foot of the Sheep Mountains, Corn Creek was a natural camping ground for those on their way to Pahranagat Valley and the town of Alamo.

Seed grasses and other edible plants in the sand dunes provided an abundance of food for the early Native Americans. Animals venturing down from the mountains to browse and drink would provide fresh meat, skins, and bone for tools. As mentioned earlier, evidence of prehistoric man can be found around every spring near Corn Creek, while in the foothills of the Sheep Mountains, just above the dunes and springs, is a network of their ancient trails.

Warning signs on the old road from Alamo back to Corn Creek on its east end at Pahranagat Valley National Wildlife Refuge Headquarters (no visitor services). Photo: Wynne Benti

Some trails lead to nothing, while others lead to seeps of water and sheltered camps once used by these prehistoric travelers.

Leaving Corn Creek, the dirt road forks. We take the left fork, heading northwest past the sign that reads Hidden Forest. Through a maze of cacti and sage, the road ascends a moderate grade and enters a boulder-strewn wash where it winds through a forest of yucca. The desert traveler reaches a narrow portal of rock. It marks the natural boundary of the wonderful arboreal domain lying beyond. The line of demarcation is sharply drawn. To the west extends a vast expanse of desert, ridged, and broken by successive ranges of sterile mountains. To the east, rise the wooded heights of the Sheep Range and the Hidden Forest.

Towering above the Hidden Forest is rugged Hayford Peak (9,912 feet). This remote mountain has long been a favorite with local climbers because of its difficulty and the spectacular view from its summit.

Passing the Hidden Forest Road (about 15 miles from Corn Creek Station), the scenery becomes more unusual. The first effect is one of isolation. Save for the sighing of the wind and the occasional call of a bird, silence is so complete and unbroken that it makes a profound impression on one whose ears have become accustomed to sounds of human activity. Silhouetted against the sky are twisted yucca and windswept rocky outcrops. Broken, rocky ground stretches from the Sheep Mountains on the east to the Desert Range on the west. Ahead the dirt track stretches invitingly, sometimes disappearing momentarily from view, only to reappear as one travels on.

As White Sage Flat is approached, the landscape begins to flatten. About 5.8 miles north of the turnoff to Hidden Forest, in the bottom of White Sage Flat, there is a branch road leading east and marked with a sign that says White Rock Spring. It is approximately four miles to the spring area and it makes a lovely hike in the cooler months of the year.

Low, grayish shrubs grow profusely and give the desert floor the appearance of a large billowing dust cloud. At the edge of the flat is a dry lake. This small playa gives evidence of having been at least an occasional camping spot for early Native people. Scattered flint and chert chippings are found along its powdery shoreline. This modem road follows the very same route that was used for untold centuries by game animals and nomadic people to pass back and forth from Pahranagat Valley to the Las Vegas Valley. Precious water sources were found along the way and their locations were remembered for future reference. About 6.2 miles past the White Rock Spring Road, the road forks. The left fork heads west toward Indian Springs along Highway 95, but this route is forbidden given the presence of a bombing range.

We turn right (north), and passing Dead Horse Ridge and Saddle Mountain of the East Desert Range on the right, the dirt road

Pahranagat Wildlife Refuge is a lush oasis amidst Nevada's basin and range with excellent viewing of wildlife including native and migratory birds. Photo: Wynne Benti

climbs another series of ridges, crossing Sheep Pass, then drops down into a large valley, surrounded by rugged mountains. A large dry lake bed, its shoreline clustered with clumps of sand dunes, covers two-thirds of the area. This is Cabin Springs Dry Lake which served as an Indian hunting and camping area for centuries.

Once, a violent desert rainstorm took us completely by surprise here. In less than thirty minutes, the bottom of the lake filled with water from shore to shore to a depth of about two feet. As abruptly as it started, the storm blew over. The sun came out and for a short time I got a privileged glimpse back into history when the desert lakes were brimming with water. Within an hour, every trace of the water had retreated into the porous earth and the lake bed was again a windswept desert playa.

Sadly, this serene valley was once used as a strafing range and the bullet-riddled wrecks of target automobiles glimmer on the far horizon. Large shell casings and various aircraft debris also litter the ground. Crossing the hard surface of the old lake (if dry - be careful here as you don't want to get stuck in the mud), or circumventing the east shore of the dry lake, the terrain begins to change. Low hills give way to weathered outcrops of grey rocks, so misshapen that the formations resemble eerie animals. Thousands of erosion holes give the visitor an impression of being watched by myriad owls, hence the name Owl Valley. The road eventually makes its descent into Pahranagat Valley. If it were not for the houses and paved streets which come into view, reality would have been left far behind in this beautiful desert dreamland.

DIRECTIONS

From Las Vegas, take Highway 95 north approximately 23 miles to the signed exit Desert National Wildlife Refuge at Corn Creek Station Road. Turn right (east) and follow a good graded dirt road 4.1 miles to the signed Alamo/Mormon Well Road junction just past the Corn Creek Ranger Station. Turn left on the Alamo Valley Road, which later merges with Old Creek Road at its northern end, and follow it north to Highway 93, just south of the Pahranagat National Wildlife Refuge. Make a left on Highway 93 and continue a few miles north to Alamo. The graded dirt roads are in good to fair condition. Be sure to have a full tank of gas when you begin this drive, as the next available fuel will be along Highway 93.

Recommended basic maps: AAA Nevada/Utah road map; Benchmark Maps Nevada Road & Recreation Atlas. Check individual topographic maps for more detailed information.

SAWMILL SPRINGS

For many years I had searched for Sawmill Springs in the Sheep Mountains. I finally gave up and those springs became a place on my list of "someday trips." It took the diligence of my son Jim, and husband Jimmy, to find the elusive site. I had always looked on the west side of the mountains. They found it on the east side.

So, with a detailed map drawn by Jim and an enthusiastic bevy of friends in their four-wheel drives, we headed for the coolness of the mountains. For a few miles, the dirt road was moderately rough. Then it got so bad I wondered if my jeep would stay in one piece. As we made our way up this remote, winding trail we sighted a huge clump of greenery to our left. This verdant oasis was, of course, a desert spring, but not the spring we were seeking. The final destination was still sixteen miles further.

Soon cactus, yucca, and Span mountainside and we knew we were nearing the end of the trail. We followed the rutted track as it climbed higher and higher. Suddenly, ahead of us was a deep, shadowed wash. We descended cautiously.

Desert washes often contain sights seen nowhere else. The washes en route to Sawmill Spring have waterfalls carved from stone, natural staircases, and fossils. Desert storms have sent flash floods thundering down the canyons, exposing the roots of towering trees like skeletons. On the edges of this wash we found two mescal pits. Ancient nomadic Indians used fire pits for roasting the center of the agave or mescal plant, their prime food source. Remains of the ancient roasting pits are scattered across the desert. With its high crumbling walls, this wash was a great place to explore,

Exploring the ruins of the old sawmill

but if we were to find Sawmill Springs we had to forge ahead.

Climbing out of the wash the road all but disappeared and when it finally did become distinct, it also became awful. It was so incredibly bad I decided it would be a miracle if I managed to drive the next few miles without damage.

Finally, we were there and it was lovely. The water attracts a multitude of birds and the trees were so tall they blocked out the sunlight, leaving us in deep shadows. We found an old corral and the remains of many years accumulation of wood shavings and sawdust. There was also much evidence that our early Indians visited the spring. Of course, water was always their destination and Sawmill Springs was no exception. We spread our lunch out on an old board and threw crumbs to the birds hovering around us and perching in the surrounding trees to watch us eat.

Above us towered Hayford Peak. It was this peak that prompted my husband and son to find Sawmill Springs, as the trail is the one leading closest to the base of the peak. As we looked at the snow-capped mountain, I was amazed to think they had scaled the heights to the summit several times.

The spring got its name from the sawmill operated there in the 1890's by J.M. Thomas. Though the buildings and machinery are long since gone, the entire area offers much to draw explorers in four-wheel drive vehicles. There are many mescal pits, caves and several other springs in the same area. It is a rugged but very rewarding trip.

DIRECTIONS

From Las Vegas take Highway 95 north, approximately 23 miles to the Desert National Wildlife Refuge/Com Creek Station Road. Turn right (east) and follow a good dirt road 4.1 miles to the signed Alamo/Mormon Well Road junction just past the Corn Creek Ranger Station. There is a small interpretive display and a guest register book. Turn right on Mormon Well Road, which is good graded dirt. Conventional cars will have no problem navigating it. Drive generally east, then north approximately 33 miles to the Sawmill Road. Park at the junction of the two roads. The approximate one mile walk to the remains of the mill is a pleasant respite from the long dirt road drive.

Camping is permitted within 100 feet of any road (without driving off-road) in the refuge. Do not camp within one quarter mile of any spring. Not only is it against Refuge regulations, but human activity disrupts the wildlife that makes the area their home. Further information on the Sheep Mountains can be obtained by contacting the Desert National Wildlife Refuge office in Las Vegas.

Recommended basic maps: AAA Nevada/Utah road map; Benchmark Maps Nevada Road & Recreation Atlas. Check individual topographic maps for more detailed information.

WARSHIELD CANYON

The rain fell. A soft mist wet the face of the alkaline canyon. Under a low-hanging ledge or rock the ancient Pueblo Indians carved an intricate series of petroglyphs upon the smooth, dark wall of the cliff. The zigzag of lightning, a replica of the shaman's staff, a carefully worked reed, a graceful bighorn sheep, all these symbols were painstakingly etched into the hard stone of the sheltering ledge. In the depths of the canyon, on a slab of tumbled sandstone, a most unusual offering had been completed. Circles were cut deeply into the surface of the stone. In each circle symmetrical designs were placed, creating the look of a large war shield. Around the edge of this fallen rock deep cuts had been made at regular intervals. What was the message of this strange stone offering? Only the sealed pages of history know the answer to the secrets of this twisting, hidden canyon.

Today the hum of activity is stilled. Only the bird calls from the marsh below disturb the silence. Although it has been centuries since the ancient ones inhabited the canyon, the fine examples of their work are as clear as if they were made yesterday. Some say Warshield Canyon is haunted, for the ever-blowing wind that wafts through the narrow chasm makes strange eerie sounds.

A muffled whisper, a low murmur, even the echo of a faint laugh can be heard if you listen closely enough. Many tales, have been handed down through the ages, tales embellished by vivid imagination with each telling. Here is one:

The year was 1920 and spring had been late arriving. A damp chill permeated the air. Two men huddled around the red glow of a

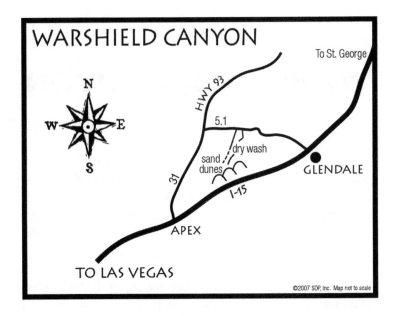

tiny fire that did little to alleviate the cold. A stray calf had led them into this maze of steep canyon walls. As the tongue of the flames leaped higher, an astonishing sight greeted their eyes. High above the sandy floor of the canyon, wedged tightly into a narrow crevice, were what appeared to be hundreds of glittering stones.

A bonanza of precious gems! A king's ransom in diamonds, topaz, aquamarines, rubies! Oh, truly great fortune was within their reach! Scrambling and clawing, they finally made their way up the vertical wall. With trembling hands they grabbed for the sparkling treasure.

When they opened their tightly clenched fists, they held only arrowheads in a kaleidoscope of colors, with sizes varying from an infinitesimal bird point to a spear tip three inches long. Disgusted, sick at heart, the men threw the ancient artifacts to the ground, trampling them into the earth.

Warshield Canyon petroglyphs

In the years that followed, many have searched unsuccessfully for the crevice that conceals the cache of Indian relics. Many, too, have theorized why the arrowheads were in the narrow crevice perched more than a hundred feet above ground.

Perhaps this mysterious canyon was a ceremonial ground and the arrowheads were shot into the crack as an offering to the Great Spirit in return for good luck in the hunt, or for the ample rain, or for the abundance of seasonal plants that year. Or perhaps, the tale is only a gem of someone's imagination. We will never know for sure.

Petroglyphs adorn almost every wall in the side canyons that branch off Warshield Canyon and they are of every variety. Bighorn sheep, antlered deer, lizards, turtles, root systems, men armed with spears, grids, sun symbols, and the most impressive warshields from which the canyon derives its name still remain for visitors to wonder about as they walk the rocky labyrinth of Warshield Canyon.

Petroglyphs occur most frequently in the west. In Nevada, alone, more than one hundred and fifty sites have been recorded, and no doubt twice that amount remains unrecorded. Many petroglyph sites show long, continual use, as if tribal migration was frequent and the writings were made by one tribe to be understood by another. It is assumed that the sites in southern Nevada were in some ways associated with hunting and water supply. There is also wide evidence of religious significance. Perhaps it might even have been a medicine man who created the interesting symbols.

In most sites there is no evidence that there was ever a permanent camp there. They evidently inhabited the vicinity, but not the actual site. Most frequently used areas in southern Nevada were the steep-walled canyons, patina-coated boulders, and the dark face of sandstone escarpments. In many instances, a spring or water preserve is found nearby, supporting a theory that petroglyphs told of good hunting territory or ideal ambush placements for stalking big game. There is an absence of these writings where game did not abound.

A fair amount of doodling is included in most petroglyph sites, but for the most part, the designs are the deliberate and planned expressions of prehistoric people. What people were responsible for this rock art? Our earliest cultures in Nevada were the Basketmaker and the Pueblo, although a prehistoric northern Paiute culture may also have been responsible. Perhaps it was a combination of many groups. The petroglyphs' origin remains somewhat of a mystery.

The petroglyph designs are diverse. They exclude anything relating to seed gathering, fishing or rabbit hunting. Frequently found are pictures of large game being pursued by a hunter complete with an atlatl dart. Often included are deer, bighorn sheep, and antelope. Small animals are also drawn in profusion, with the lizard, scorpion, and snake being the most common.

The brown-coated rocks and cliffs are often covered with spirals, grids, reeds, and sun disk circles. Stick men, rain symbols, and circles within circles are almost demonic. Upturned hands are interpreted to signify good luck, while hands with the fingers cast down are thought to be a danger sign or a symbol of fear.

Bird tracks, birds, and claw marks play an important part in these intricate drawings. Zigzag lines and a remarkable likeness to a ladder are common. Petroglyphs were often carved on single rocks scattered over a large area (such as those found at Fort Paiute) rather than in one central location. When exposed to the elements sun, rain, and wind, the petroglyphs fade considerably. If they are placed on the sheltered side of a canyon wall, they remain as clear as the day they were created.

At Kane Springs, a most unusual petroglyph occurs. It is that of a padre standing in a crude two-wheeled cart. An engrossing study of these ancient writings can be made by visiting any or all of the following sites:

Red Spring in Calico Basin near Red Rock; Mouses Tank in Valley of Fire near Overton; Atlatl Rock in Valley of Fire; Keyhole Canyon off Boulder City.

DIRECTIONS

For Warshield Canyon, take Interstate 15 north from Las Vegas to the Great Basin National Park/Ely cutoff (Highway 93). Drive approximately 31 miles to the Glendale/Warm Springs Road, and turn right toward the Arrow Canyon Range. Go 5.1 miles to a wide, deep wash and turn right. Follow the wash to a sand dune. Park and follow the foothill of the mountain on the left side of a dune to a canyon on the right about three-quarter or one mile hike.

Recommended basic maps: AAA Nevada/Utah road map; Benchmark Maps Nevada Road & Recreation Atlas. Check individual topographic maps for more detailed information.

MEADOW VALLEY WASH

The Meadow Valley Wash stretches from Moapa Valley to Caliente. It climbs up steep volcanic escarpments, and gains summits, only to plunge downward to dry lake beds overgrown with salt grass and cactus. To the north rise sculptured rose-colored cliffs outlined against the sky of deepest blue. The great wash is bounded with abrupt and seemingly unscalable faults.

A few tiny settlements were once scattered along the narrow banks of the Muddy River. Now only the gnarled forms of patriarchal cottonwood trees redeem their settings from a category of desolation. A lone shack, some rusted farm equipment, a corral or two proclaim the fact that once the settlements had greater dignity.

With each sharp turn in the road only the unknown seems to lie ahead, stretching to a skyline forever in the distance. To the south, a volcanic cinder cone adds a somber touch to the lure of the beckoning horizon. Vermillion cliffs fade into a distance, their bold contours softened by a pale lavender haze. As the road ascends, a view of the ribbon-like Muddy River lends itself to the scenery. Willows, cottonwoods, and wild plants in abundance crowd the sandy banks. Bird songs echo in the otherwise silent valley.

Prehistoric people were the first inhabitants of Meadow Valley Wash for upon the many mesa fingers is evidence of their habitation. Above the old railroad siding of Rox, on a hard floor of desert varnish, is a rare and intricate rock design left by early Indians. Many rock circles, metates and ma burned by occupants of long ago. Near the railroad tracks on the side of a precipitous cliff are a great number of petroglyphs and pictographs.

Meadow Valley Wash

In a narrow canyon, a cliff juts two hundred feet above the sandy floor of the wash. In this volcanic tuff cliff is the mouth of an ancient cave once inhabited by prehistoric man. Four to five feet above the entrance is a group of colorful, rare pictographs. In front of the mouth, large rocks have fallen into place. This slide is so massive that in some areas it touches the cave roof near the forty-foot wide entrance. The sloping floor of the interior was divided into three levels, separated by low stone walls built by the early Pueblo culture.

Etna Cave was explored by archaeologists in 1935. Many specimens of tools, pottery, matting and weapons were unearthed, but the most spectacular find was sixty-two woven twine sandals, the most ever found in a single dig. A large variety of cordage made from hemp, yucca, juniper bark and milkweed were unearthed. Fragments of a most unusual netting, bundles of Indian Hemp, and two torches were also found. Many fragments of coiled basketry

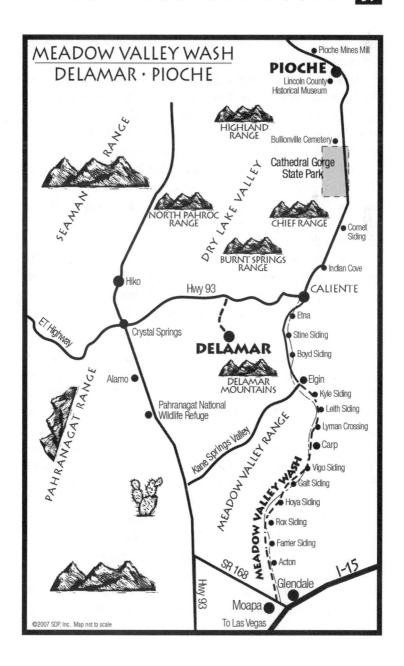

MEADOW VALLEY WASH
DELAMAR · PIOCHE

Pioche Mines Mill

PIOCHE

Lincoln County
Historical Museum

HIGHLAND
RANGE

Bullionville Cemetery

Cathedral Gorge
State Park

SEAMAN RANGE

NORTH PAHROC
RANGE

DRY LAKE VALLEY

CHIEF RANGE

Comet
Siding

BURNT SPRINGS
RANGE

Indian Cove

Hiko

Hwy 93

CALIENTE

ET Highway

Crystal Springs

DELAMAR

Etna

Stine Siding

Boyd Siding

PAHRANAGAT RANGE

Alamo

DELAMAR
MOUNTAINS

Elgin

Kyle Siding

Pahranagat National
Wildlife Refuge

Leith Siding

Lyman Crossing

Kane Springs Valley

MEADOW VALLEY RANGE

Carp

Vigo Siding

MEADOW VALLEY WASH

Galt Siding

Hoya Siding

Rox Siding

Farrier Siding

SR 168

Acton

I-15

Hwy 93

Glendale

Moapa

To Las Vegas

©2007 SDP, Inc. Map not to scale

were found, but only one complete basket, now known as the Fremont River specimen.

Jedediah Smith was the earliest known explorer of Meadow Valley Wash in 1826. In 1858, scouts for the Mormon Church sought new areas for settlement. Later in 1863, colonists were sent from St. George, Utah to start settling the Meadow Valley as well as Clover, Eagle, and Spring Valleys farther north.

In 1864 rich ore was discovered in the Pioche mining district. That discovery set off a run of traffic through the winding wash and in July of that same year the Meadow Valley Mining Corporation was founded. Their mines produced more than 100 million dollars in bullion.

Now, mining in Meadow Valley is at a standstill. The dust that once followed the wagon trains has settled to the ground. Activity is limited to a few working ranches and a railroad siding or two in the wash. It is a place of peaceful solitude and natural beauty.

DIRECTIONS

This route is definitely not recommended during periods of rain, particularly during the summer thunderstorm season. Meadow Valley Wash drains a huge area of southern Nevada, and although the weather may look fine, storms far to the north may cause the area to flood. From Las Vegas take Interstate 15 north approximately 47 miles to Glendale (Exit 90). Drive 2.8 miles west on State Route 168 to a dirt road heading north and following the Meadow Valley Wash. Follow the Meadow Valley Wash Road as it crosses and recrosses the railroad tracks. Eventually after about 70 miles, the road reaches the pavement at the little settlement of Elgin. The town of Caliente is only 22 miles ahead on Highway 93. Highway 93 can then be followed back to Las Vegas.

Recommended basic maps: AAA Nevada/Utah road map; Benchmark Maps Nevada Road & Recreation Atlas. Check individual topographic maps for more detailed information.

DELAMAR

Just a three-hour drive from Las Vegas is the old mining camp of Delamar. As popular as it may be, Delamar is still a thrill to visit. The discovery of Delamar in the 1890s brought a great many gold and silver seekers into Lincoln County. Coming into Delamar from the upper road must have been quite a sight! Houses built of native rock, huge mine structures, numerous stores and saloons, even a church or two, were all settled in this small valley.

The walls of most buildings were thick, smoothly cemented and whitewashed inside and out. Roofs were made of corrugated tin and covered with dirt and stones for insulation. Until a few years ago many of the buildings were in fairly good condition after withstanding almost a century of weather. Sadly, Delamar has been vandalized over the years, and what a pity it is only to be able to imagine how it must have been.

In the beginning, the camp was called Ferguson, in honor of two brothers of that name who first discovered gold there in Monkey Wrench Wash in 1891. More than twenty-five million dollars worth of gold was produced from 1892 to 1909 when Captain John R. Delamar decided to dismantle the entire enterprise. In 1907, there were about thirty-six miles of underground workings, with shafts up to 1,300 feet deep. More than five hundred miners worked there at its height.

East of Delamar in the long canyon was the April Fool Mine. It produced so much ore that a ten-stamp mill was built there and the extraction rate of ninety-five percent was accomplished by means of two-thirds on the plates and the other one-third by cyanization.

The old mill at Delamar

The old Magnolia Mine in Helen Wash just north of the camp was the site of the first discovery of gold. At that time the ore had to be sent all the way to Hiko for processing. Remains of the mills and tailing piles at Delamar show that there was much activity and ample machinery. The mill was first operated by steam power. Later, it was changed to electricity generated at Stine on the railway twelve miles away.

Water, which proved to be a problem in most desert mining camps, was brought at first from Cedar Wash, three miles east of the camp using a pumping method. As the camp expanded, more water was needed and it was eventually pumped from a well in the Meadow Valley Wash twelve miles east. This operation required a lift of 2,000 feet to three different pumping stations.

Some families, even with a scant water supply, managed to have beautiful gardens with lilacs, vines, fruit trees and vegetables. Some of the trees still grow today, as if trying to recall the memories of their industrious planters.

Stores and other large buildings must have been numerous. Some are now nothing but shells with gaping basements and many are rubble. A few years ago one hotel was still standing, its high arched windows intact. Another building was undoubtedly a school, as the remains of swings and a flagpole gave mute evidence. The population of Delamar was almost 1,000 in 1900, but in 1902 most of the townspeople moved on to a new boom in Tonopah.

Delamar has two cemeteries. The inscriptions on the tombstones show that most of the dead were victims of quartz dust from the dry mills and the mines that were even dustier, a dust equal to finely powdered glass. Is it any wonder the camp's nickname was The Widow Maker? At one time there were more than four hundred widows living in Delamar.

As you walk through the sad, vandalized camp, you may still find relics of the past: a square nail, a shriveled old boot, bits of purple glass, even shreds of old mail order catalogs. There are many ghost towns that are easier to get to and with which we are more familiar. However, they are not quite as interesting as Delamar. Even in its contemporary state of decay, the mines and the town located in the deep valley make such a beautiful picture.

The trip is a very fulfilling one and is best in spring or early fall. The dirt roads are good except the final one into Delamar. It is usually passable using a little caution. Take a camera, as well, for it is a picturesque adventure.

The author's father mined gold at Delamar

DIRECTIONS

From Las Vegas, take Interstate 15 north to Highway 93, the Great Basin Highway/Ely cutoff. The road to Delamar is on the right, 112 miles from the Interstate, and about 16 miles before you get to Caliente, Delamar is about 12 miles south along the gravel, then dirt, road.

Recommended basic maps: AAA Nevada/Utah road map; Benchmark Maps Nevada Road & Recreation Atlas. Check USGS topo maps for more detailed information.

CATHEDRAL GORGE AND BULLIONVILLE

One mile north of Panaca is another of Nevada's state park gems. Surrounded by scattered grasslands, pinyon, juniper and sage, is a valley of eroded cliffs, an orange-ochre colored badland known as Cathedral Gorge. Imagine an underground cave turned inside out, its delicately carved stalagmites, like the pipes on a church organ, rise into blue sky to touch the clouds which helped create them. It is a quiet place where the wind carries voices across the grasslands, through the trees to the cliffs where they vanish into the fantastic shapes. Walking along one of the many nature trails, you look behind you but there is no one, just the wind playing games. Nature trails meander throughout the entire badlands, in and out of narrow slotted canyons shaped by nature into spectacular symmetrical forms.

These formations, called lakebed deposits, began as the remains of an ancient lake more than a million years old, that once covered the region from Caliente to Panaca. Geologists call this particular grouping of deposits the Panaca Formation. Nature-- the wind, rain and melting snows put the finishing touches on the lake sediments by slowly carving the fantastic shapes we see today. There is a campground and many nature trails.

Just over the hills to the east is the site of Bullionville, a mill town founded in 1869 following the discovery of silver at Pioche about ten miles north. In the early 1920s, Mrs. Godbe,

Opposite: Andy Zdon at Cathedral Gorge
Above: Grave at Bullionville. Photos: Wynne Benti

married to the reduction plant manager at Bullionville was riding her horse through the grasslands and came upon Cathedral Gorge. Soon it became a popular spot for picnics. Parties would perform vaudeville-style plays with the mudlike organ pipes as a backdrop. Word of this wonderful place spread and by 1924, Nevada's Governor James G. Scrugham designated it as a park and by 1935, it became one of Nevada's first four official state parks.

Little remains of Bullionville today. The old townsite is across the highway from Cathedral Gorge. Bullionville was founded in the early 1870's by John Ely and W. Raymond who moved their stamp mill from Hiko to the site. The easy access to water turned Bullionville into the primary center

Geologist Andy Zdon at Cathedral Gorge Photo: Wynne Benti

for processing ore for the mines at Pioche, up the road about ten miles. When a water works was built at Pioche by the mid 1870s, Bullionville's mills moved to Pioche and by the 1890s, the town, which once boasted five ore mills, 500 residents and the first iron foundry in eastern Nevada was all but a ghost town. Just north of the Cathedral Gorge entrance on a grassy knoll above the highway, is Bullionville's well-preserved cemetery.

DIRECTIONS

Take I-15 north from Las Vegas to Hwy 93. Head north on Hwy. 93 to Alamo, Caliente and Panaca. One mile north of Panaca turn left at the entrance to Cathedral Gorge State Park. The old town site of Bullionville is just across the highway from the park entrance. An alternate route is the Old Road to Alamo across Desert National Wildlife Refuge.

Recommended basic maps: AAA Nevada/Utah road map; Benchmark Maps Nevada Road & Recreation Atlas. Check individual topographic maps for more detailed information.

IN AND AROUND PIOCHE

Mines are not usually found in accessible places. When they do survive the prospect stage, a town grows up around the mine following the contour of the terrain. Pioche was no exception to the rule.

Pioche. What a fitting name for a mining camp. It is the French word for pick axe. Coincidentally, a French banker named R. L. Pioche from San Francisco financially backed the Pioche mines in their early development.

Many mining camps in Nevada were short of duration. A flurry of hopes was followed by disappointment, and the exodus of all residents. Pioche was not one of those, for it is still a lovely town. The old, well-kept homes have trees and flowers, a blend of mining camp and modem town. Water is piped from springs located in the mountains eight miles away. An ample supply contributes to the cozy look of most houses.

In 1874, Pioche had a population of 6,000 people. True, it has decreased a great deal, but Pioche still lives up to its glorious past. Between 1860 and 1876, the camp experienced a slump as the prices of lead and silver values began to fluctuate, but the ore deposit depth proved to extend even further than the miners originally believed, and was mined for many years. The ore zones were 1,000 to 1,500 feet deep and for safety, prospecting was done with chum drills a good distance from the working mines.

The main mines in the Pioche area were the Prince and Virginia-Louise. They have become historical landmarks. The Consolidated Ely-Valley, Raymond-Ely and Combined Metals were the biggest producers and had large modem plants with the latest equipment.

Pioche from the Aerial Tram. Photo: Wynne Benti

The Castleton plant is a good example of mining's modernization in Pioche.

The Consolidated Ely-Valley Mine had a 1,000 foot vertical shaft that was very costly to put in, but more than three hundred tons of ore were shipped daily to the smelter. The surface ores were treated easily but the deep ore, lead, and zinc, were so complex that none of the smelters could extract both economically. One of the two had to be considered a total loss.

The milling and smelting of the ores were fascinating procedures. First the ore was separated into piles. Then a form of bulldozer would push each pile into ore bins. From these bins the ore was taken to a gyratory crusher via a conveyor belt that ran into a Symonds cone crusher, vibrating screens, a weightometer and finally elevated to the fine ore bins. From there it passed through separate outlets and was sent to be ground even finer in the Harding ball mills. Then it was conditioned for lead flotation and processed to Faggergren cells. The tailings from all this were then pumped back for zinc conditioning. Bucket elevators then took the concentrates to the upper part of the plant where they were filtered and dumped directly into waiting railroad cars.

A most interesting building is Pioche's historic court house constructed in 1872. The cost was a staggering $ 1,000,000. It was built of brick imported from England. In 1938 the offices were moved to new buildings and the court house fell into disrepair. Thankfully, it was restored to its former condition and is open to the public.

Just below town is a cemetery known as *Boot Hill,* as most of the deceased were buried with their boots on. Many stories explain why, but the one I like best was told to me by an old miner.

"Waaal," he drawled, "If they gits up on the other side an the law's still after them, they're ready to skeedaddle."

Unmarked graves fill the public cemetery. The few with headstones tell a whole story in just a few lines. One dated 1880 reads:

"His days how few, How sudden passed away, To pay the debt, Each mortal has to pay."

On another with no date:

"Beneath this stone in soft repose, Tis laid a mothers dearest pride, A flower that scarce has waked to life, And light and beauty ere it died."

Caliente, Pioche and Panaca, three adjoining towns all rich in Nevada history, are trips you will long remember. Though Pioche is the most interesting, Caliente, too, has its charms. Railroad whistles and smoke used to permeate the air around the thick cottonwood trees surrounding Caliente, a Union Pacific Railroad town in a canyon with scenic sites. It has a little bit of everything. The hot springs just north of town are sheer delight. Several motels have pools and private baths that are wonderful

Just a block south of the end of Main Street is a sign that reads Kershaw-Ryan State Park and it is a green jewel in the desert. There are hiking trails, smooth lawns, wild grapes, palm trees, tumbling water and camping accommodations.

Traveling further north we come to Panaca, a lovely verdant farming community settled in 1864 by Francis Lee and his family. The old homes and green fields are picturesque.

The Million Dollar Court House of Pioche. Photo: Andy Zdon

Take a short side trip to Cathedral Gorge. It is like an outdoor cave complete with stalagmites. The entire area is formed of an unusual light-colored mineral, much like dried mud that the elements have shaped into spectacular architectural forms.

The roaring mining camp days of Pioche and Caliente have gone. So have the days of the burro prospectors, glory holes, and boom towns. Where once sounded the din of many voices, the thud of hard-driven pick and shovel, only the sounds of a town and its people can be heard. Such is the fate of the old west. Much has already become a mere recollection in the annals of our priceless heritage.

DIRECTIONS
Take Interstate 15 north about 20 miles to Highway 93, the Great Basin Highway, and head north. Pass by Pahranagat Lakes, Alamo, and Ash Springs. Continue on Highway 93. Caliente is about 44 miles past Ash Springs and 126 miles from the interstate. From Caliente, continue north on Highway 93 for 30 more miles to Pioche.

Recommended basic maps: AAA Nevada/Utah road map; Benchmark Maps Nevada Road & Recreation Atlas. Check individual topographic maps for more detailed information.

WHIPPLE CAVE

While much of Nevada has been explored on the surface in the search for precious minerals, most of the ground beneath is relatively unknown. Many believe the sterile limestone mountain ranges are honeycombed with great caverns. Who is to say that they are wrong?

Sometimes there is no way to tell if the solid ground on which you stand is truly solid. Is it instead, merely a crust covering stygian labyrinths that have never seen the light of day? Many of these fantastic realms have been discovered by accident. Someone stands on a spot where the crust has worn thin, breaks through and tumbles into the depths of an alien world.

A noteworthy discovery of this type occurred more than 125 years ago when a rancher from Sunnyside, Nevada was climbing the slope of an unnamed peak eight miles northeast of the town. He came upon a great sink hole forty feet in diameter. In the dim light below, he could see what appeared to be the bottom of the pit, where a large tunnel disappeared into the mountain depths.

He returned several days later with a friend and a rope ladder. The cave was an immense cavern, perhaps the largest known west of the Rocky Mountains. The biggest chamber was over a half-mile in length with a roof more than a hundred feet high. For nearly thirty years after its discovery, the cavern remained practically unknown, even to residents of White Pine County where it is found.

Whipple Cave was named in honor of J. L. Whipple of Sunnyside, who installed strong wooden ladders, making the cavern accessible to the public. With several features that are unique, Whipple Cave is worthy of a visit although it is in a rather remote location. The country is flat and barren. Its monotony is relieved by the White Pine Mountains that are timbered and powdered with snow, and the rugged desert ranges, fading purple in the distant haze. The desolation of the broad valley is intensified by a few lush fields.

Fine alluvial dust lies thick upon the roads and rises in a cloud behind any passing vehicle. Some three miles north of the site of Sunnyside, a road branches to the east and leads over a sage-covered plain toward a serrated chain of mountains. The gentle slope gradually increases to a steep grade. It reaches the brink of a great hole in the mountains which is spanned by a natural bridge of limestone.

Once inside the cavern, it takes a few moments for ones eyes to become accustomed to the dim light. As this happens, the vast proportions of the cave are revealed. Fifty feet overhead a vaulted roof is visible, as it fades away into stygian gloom. Even with good lighting, the eerie landscape outside the perimeter of the glow is deceptive. Distances could be five feet or fifteen. The true immensity of the cavern hits with great force when all visual contact with the roof and walls is lost when nothing but black void extends beyond the spot where you are standing. It is then possible to know how it would have felt 125 years ago when the only light was a lantern or torch that suddenly went out.

About a quarter-mile inside the caverns entrance, the skeleton of a large wolf was found on top of a boulder. It was one of Whipple Caves most puzzling riddles. Beside it lay the skull of a mountain sheep, the softer bones chewed away, the resistant frontal bones scored by those long, sharp teeth. Is it possible the sheep, chased by the wolf plunged into the deep hole to escape; and that the wolf followed and paid the penalty, death by starvation or the fall itself?

With its enormous size, Whipple Cave is just as interesting as Lehman Caves, though its formations are less extensive. There is at least one feature that surpasses its prototype at Great Basin National Park, a stalactite of giant proportions extending from floor to ceiling, with a diameter of about seventy feet. Fluted and crenulated by

Inside Whipple Cave

the slow deposits of ages, that impressive megalith, towering like the column of a temple to a vaulted dome far overhead is an awe-inspiring sight.

With certain variations of details, formations in Whipple Cave are similar to those of other caverns. There are masses of icicle-like crystal pendants hanging from the ceiling, stalactites resembling clusters of grapes, and irregular nodules that look like balls of pop-

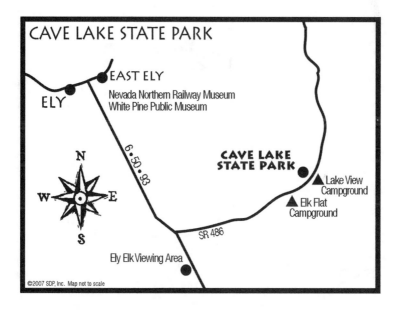

corn. Curtains of onyx through which transmitted light reveals patterns of rare artistry, columns wound into whorls and spirals like pulled taffy, and a fountain turned to stone, are among the wonderful formations found throughout the caverns. These, with other strange and beautiful bric-a-brac too numerous to mention, pass in review as one moves through the caverns. The strange realm into which you have entered is a journey of true adventure.

DIRECTIONS

From Las Vegas take Interstate 15 north about 20 miles to Great Basin National Park/Ely Road (Highway 93). Follow Highway 93 about 85 miles north just past Ash Springs to a junction with Highway 375 (also known as the Extra Terrestrial Highway). Follow Highway 375 west one mile, then turn north on Highway 318 and drive approximately 67 miles to a dirt road heading east. Whipple Cave is reached by driving about five miles east on the dirt road, then south to the cave.

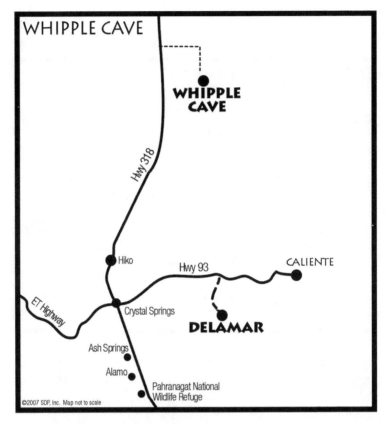

WHIPPLE CAVE

Hwy 318

Hiko

Hwy 93

CALIENTE

Crystal Springs

ET Highway

DELAMAR

Ash Springs

Alamo

Pahranagat National
Wildlife Refuge

©2007 SDP, Inc. Map not to scale

For further adventure, Highway 318 can be followed north toward Highway 6 and Ely. When at Ely, consider a visit to the Ward Charcoal Ovens State Historic Monument, and watch for wildlife at the Ely Elk Viewing Area. One can also drive five miles south of Ely and turn left (east) on State Route 486, following it to Cave Lake State Park. There is camping at the state park. Also, visit the Visitors Center, the White Pine Public Museum, and the Nevada Northern Railway Museum.

Recommended basic maps: AAA Nevada/Utah road map; Benchmark Maps Nevada Road & Recreation Atlas. Check individual topographic maps for more detailed information.

LEHMAN CAVES

Caves have long fascinated us. To prehistoric men they offered shelter. Later, Native Americans, prospectors, and travelers were known to use the caves as hideouts, shelters, or storage places. Until more recent times, however, intruders into this dark deep environment seldom went far beyond the entrance or first chamber. Torch light was unreliable and a breeze might extinguish the flame, leaving its bearer in total darkness. It was for this reason, that the vast array of flashing gems and glittering statuary that adorn Nevada's caverns was left untouched.

It was in 1883 when the first of these caves was discovered by a lone prospector named Ab (short for Absalom) Lehman, who was guiding his horse down the east slope of Mount Wheeler into Spring Valley. The metallic click of iron-shod hooves on limestone suddenly gave way to a splintering crash as his horse plunged earthward, pinning his master underneath. Lehman was astonished. Extricating himself, he began to pry away the rocks and turf surrounding the small hole in the mountainside. A cold wind from its black interior told him he was standing directly over a large cavern, the extent and character of which could only be determined later with the use of ropes and lanterns.

Subsequent exploration by Lehman, for whom the cave was named, revealed a series of chambers and galleries fairly bristling with stalactite formations, weird, beautiful, and grotesque. Lehman had heard of several caves back east, but prior to the painful spill on the mountainside he had not suspected the existence of any similar cavern west of the Mississippi River. Located in a remote area where population was sparse, Lehman Caves were relatively unknown until the creation of Great Basin National Park, even though Lehman Caves National Monument was created in 1922.

About sixty miles from Ely, Nevada, is the town of Baker, which is six miles northeast of the caves. From this place is an excellent view of Wheeler Peak, at 13,063 feet, the second highest peak in the state. Remarkable, too, are the three distinct zones of vegetation so plainly visible. In the foreground, a level expanse of sagebrush extends above the low foothills and merges with the timber belt girdling the mountainside in a broad green sash. Bare in summer with only a few remnant patches of snow, the higher slopes converge to the summit where few varieties of plant life can exist.

Lehman Caves are located some distance below the heavy timber where a few scrubby pinyons mark a transition from the desert to the domain of stately conifers. Here, through countless ages the cave was formed. Groundwater from snow and rain on the slopes above, carrying lime in solution, dripped from its ceiling to form a myriad of strange accretions which have made the cavern famous.

When the guided tour starts, the first view is of irregular limestone walls. There is a distinct chill to the air, whose temperature is said to vary but two or three degrees throughout the year. Next to be seen are smooth, elongated forms of stone that contrast sharply with the broken surfaces from which they hang. Rising from the floor, carpeted with the dust of ages, arise pinnacles of similar composition that bear a striking resemblance to unfinished statues. Yet this sight is scant preparation for the fantastic scene that lies ahead. A winding corridor emerges into the first of a long series of chambers that extend nearly a mile underground, an amazing subterranean palace! This illusion is strengthened by the Fairy Rosebush, a delicate formation resembling its ephemeral namesake that thrives on daylight and sunshine.

A forest of stalagmites, masses of stalactites varying in size from a darning needle to a large tree trunk, fluted columns from floor to vaulted ceiling, spirals, frozen waterfalls and delicate portals, such are the amazing spectacles confronting the beholder at every turn. Imagination needs no spur to see fantastic likenesses everywhere. Thus, the visitor wanders through a labyrinth where fact and fancy merge. One finds himself peering through the gloom, half expecting to catch a glimpse of a shadowy form scurrying away through the colonnaded chamber. But, these fantasies are dispelled by the guides account of the cavern's making.

According to scientific reports, an underground stream flowed through a crack in the limestone, leeching out great quantities of chemicals and excavating a huge void. Later, ground water carrying lime in solution, dripped from the roof of the cave. Each drop evaporated and left its content of solid substance to build stalactites that hang like icicles. Other drops, falling to the floor, built up the stalagmites in a similar manner. In many cases, these joined to form columns, which in time were greatly enlarged and fluted to become more ornate than any gothic cathedral. Frequently the water was diverted laterally and built up translucent draperies. A striking example is seen in the Navajo blanket, in which alternate bands of white and amber suggest this appropriate name.

Passing from chamber to chamber, through tortuous passageways and corridors, one's sense of direction is completely confused. Unexpected, then, is the appearance of a flight of stairs leading upward. Eyes that have become accustomed to feeble lighting are decidedly uncomfortable in the blaze of sunlight at the exit. The feeling is like awakening from a gorgeous, fantastic dream.

DIRECTIONS

From Las Vegas take Interstate 15 north about 20 miles to Highway 93 (Caliente/Pioche). Follow Highway 93 north about 230 miles, passing through Ash Springs, Caliente and Pioche, to the point where the road forks. The right fork goes east to Great Basin National Park and Lehman Caves. The nearest town with gas and food is Baker, Nevada. The left fork heads west to Ely, Nevada which has all facilities. Mileage from Las Vegas to Great Basin National Park is approximately 300 miles, one way. The National Park Visitor Center is open daily and offers ninety-minute cave tours (for a reasonable fee) and information. A cafe is open from Memorial Day to mid-October. There are fine campgrounds in the national park.

Recommended basic maps: AAA Nevada/Utah road map; Benchmark Maps Nevada Road & Recreation Atlas. Check individual topographic maps for more detailed information.

THE EXTRA TERRESTRIAL HIGHWAY

For those who believe in unidentified flying objects, the Extra Terrestrial or ET Highway is the place to view the inexplicable. This lonely rural Nevada highway is famous for secret government projects, sightings of glowing, moving objects in a multitude of colors, little green men, and other pulsating and puzzling anomalies seen most often in the night skies.

Beginning in the south at the lovely ranching community of Crystal Springs, the ET highway ends ninety-eight miles to the north at an abandoned hot springs settlement called Warm Springs on Highway 6, which can be followed west to Highway 95 at Tonopah, then south again to Las Vegas.

The highway runs along the east side of Nellis Air Force Base, Yucca Mountain, the Nevada Test Site, Area 51, and the Tonopah Test Range, which together encompass millions of desert acreage historically used during the 20th century for the testing of hi-tech military weaponry. There are no street signs along ET indicating that a military base even exists anywhere in the area, but don't be fooled. The perimeter of "Area 51" is well-secured and monitored visually and physically. The security force is rumored to be made up of former veterans who served in such elite U.S. military forces as the Navy Seals. They are authorized to use deadly force to ensure that the base remains secured. We have seen them for real along the

ET highway in unmarked champagne-colored Ford F-150 trucks, wearing navy blue tee-shirts with the word security printed across the back.

Close to the base and surrounded by BLM (Bureau of Land Management public lands) is a cattle ranch. Most Nevada ranching families go back many generations and established their private holdings over a hundred years ago. These ranches can be seen all over the countryside of rural Nevada, sometimes the only group of structures for miles. Please respect their privacy.

Perhaps the most famous destination along the ET Highway is Rachel, Nevada, a small rural town originally founded to service the mining operations at the old Union Carbide Tungsten Mine across the highway at Tempiute, now closed. Rachel is the closest civilian town to "Area 51" not on the test site, located approximately 28.2 miles north of Groom Lake, the location of some of the military's most classified research and testing. In his book, "The Area 51 & S-4 Handbook" author, Chuck Clark says that no one knows what Area 51 is actually called. The current numerical reference, Area 51, is a leftover from the long ago days of atomic testing.

Though it's a trailer town, easily moved in and out to follow the mining activity, Rachel has all of the amenities, not the fanciest but certainly one of the friendliest: a restaurant, motel, mini-mart with gas station, and RV sites with hookups. Do not expect to get a room at the Little A'Le'Inn motel without a reservation since Rachel is a popular destination spot visited by tourists from all over the world.

The Little A'Le'Inn combines the classic rural atmosphere of a Central Nevada restaurant and bar with alien-UFO paraphernalia. Where else can you have a beer and good hamburger while peering into the black eyes of a replica alien from FOX Broadcasting Company's alien autopsy special? There is a fabulous collection of UFO photographs, ET Highway and alien collectibles, and an out of this world gift store (pardon the pun) that has everything one could ever possibly want—little green and silver men, bumper stickers,

mouse pads, books, UFO spaceship model kits, and a varied assortment of excellent shirts including one of the famous Groom Lake Flying Club. Just outside the restaurant is a concrete "ID4" marker commemorating the 1996 premiere of the 20th Century FOX alien invasion flick, *Independence Day*.

If you love wide open spaces, this is a great way to see the best of Central Nevada's beautiful remote countryside. Colorful mesas, expansive clear blue skies, the town of Rachel with its Area 51 paraphernalia make the road trip to the ET highway a wonderful way to explore some of the best unspoiled country Nevada has to offer.

DIRECTIONS

From Las Vegas, take I-15 north to Highway 93. Exit on 93 north to Pioche. At Crystal Springs turn left on Highway 375, the Extra Terrestrial Highway. Follow to Rachel and its terminus at Warm Springs and Highway 6. To create a loop trip, turn west (left) at Warm Springs and follow Hwy. 6 to Tonopah. Turn south on Highway 95 and follow it back to Las Vegas, through Beatty, past Carrara and the Amargosa Dunes, the site of Lucky's lost whiskey-filled wagon.

Recommended basic maps: AAA Nevada/Utah road map; Benchmark Maps Nevada Road & Recreation Atlas. Check individual topographic maps for more detailed information.

TYBO'S LOST NUGGETS

In 1869, rumors reached Belmont and Manhattan, two of Nevada's roughest mining towns, that prospectors were finding big gold nuggets in the gravel wash up Hot Creek Canyon way. There was feverish excitement as every man who lost his shirt in Belmont and Manhattan began looking for transportation to the new strike.

But where in Hot Creek Canyon? Wagons carrying supplies brought news of the new gold field, but as to the exact location, only vague descriptions were available.

"Up the canyon somewhere," was the common response to any serious query. There were no roads, only Indian trails. Who needs roads anyway? Just the thought of all those gleaming nuggets could make an Indian trail look like a well-paved garden walk.

And so the stampede was on. In buckboards, on horseback, in creaking wagons and on foot, they headed for the canyon as fast as they could get together a grubstake and pack their burros.

Walt Harral was one of the first to reach the new field. From a self-styled Indian Chief called Bazdo, he learned the location of the springs in the juniper-covered heights of the Hot Creek Range. Harral went over the routes and found the springs just as old Chief Bazdo had described them. With energy stiffed by thoughts of a golden bonanza, Harral began his search for the fabled nuggets. Weeks were spent clearing a road for his wagon, traces of which can still be seen.

By 1872, the gold camp of Tybo was in full swing, but instead of being the golden lode many had claimed, it was silver that made

One of the remaining shacks at Tybo. Photo: Leslie Payne

the town boom. The silver ran 250 ounces to the one and one-half ounces of gold to the ton. It wasn't fantastically rich. Every now and then, a rich pocket would turn up that would send the mining world into a spin.

Several kilns were erected to keep an abundance of charcoal available for the busy smelters. With the forest of junipers near at hand, the set-up was considered ideal. Furnaces and mills were operating at full capacity to serve the eight large mines.

Tybo seemed destined for great things. As long as oxidized ores were treated, all went well. Disaster occurred when sulfides came in at large tonnages. Operations became so difficult that one by one the mining companies closed down and boarded up their buildings. In 1878, the Tybo Consolidated ceased operation and the town was abandoned.

At an elevation of 6,700 feet, Tybo is a scenic relic of Nevada's golden yesteryear of mining. Today, there are huge piles of slag glittering in the sun. A few weathered, gray shacks, brick foundations, and the remnants of a half dozen houses, some still in good repair, a quaint schoolhouse and a multitude of untold stories are all that

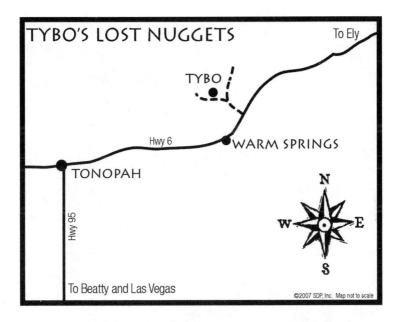

are left of Tybo's glory days. To the best of my knowledge, the source of the gold nuggets that started the rush to Tybo was never relocated. One of the many surrounding canyons may still contain the pocket of glowing nuggets, just waiting to be discovered.

DIRECTIONS

From Las Vegas, take Highway 95 to north to Tonopah approximately 210 miles. Turn east on Highway 6 and drive about 44 miles to Warm Springs. Continue on Highway 6 about ten miles past Warm Springs, then turn west on a dirt road. Tybo is about four miles up this road. Four-wheel drive recommended. Some property in Tybo is privately owned, so be sure to respect all no trespassing signs.

Recommended basic maps: AAA Nevada/Utah road map; Benchmark Maps Nevada Road & Recreation Atlas. Check individual topographic maps for more detailed information.

Florine navigates a snowy road. Photo: Leslie Payne

In, Out, and About Red Rock

FOSSIL HILL

Fossils are a link with our remote past. Rarely are they found in one complete piece. If an extinct species of camel is found, it is often just a few bones or a skull. A shell fragment is usually all that is to be found of a shellfish, while a huge tree is represented only by small leaf fragments. Yet from these bits and pieces entire plants and animals are reconstructed.

We must study living animals and plants to really understand fossils. A comparison of many vertebrate fossils with living species shows us how similar many of the now extinct ones are to the present day animal life. By reconstructing fossils it is easy for us to see the plant or animal as it was. Fossils two and a half billion years old have been found, yet they did not become abundant until six hundred million years ago.

There are ways by which a rock or fossil can be measured in years, sometimes the breakdown of radioactive elements or carbon-dating methods has been successful. Only the incomprehensible length of geological time can explain the changes in life forms and in the earth itself. By observing the occurrence of sedimentary rocks in parallel layers and noting at what rate sediments form in bays and basins, we are able to observe the first key to the long geological time scale.

Rocks are often strewn with characteristic fossils. A short distance out from Las Vegas lies several excellent examples of fossilized hills and beds. One is on the Red Rock Canyon Road, the other on the Blue Diamond Road. These fossils are essentially the same type and many beautiful specimens can be observed.

Despite its close proximity to ever-expanding Las Vegas, it is still possible to see wild horses and burros in Red Rock National Conservation Area. Photo: Leslie Payne

An excursion to the Red Rock Canyon Road region proved most rewarding as an entire bivalve (pelecypod) was found. This shell fish is similar to an oyster or clam of today. The specimen found was whole, not in fragments. Another most interesting find was a large chunk of schizocoral, also from the Permian period.

This extinct coral multiplied only by fission and lacked true septa ever. In addition, fine examples of inarticulate brachiopods or small invertebrates can be seen on many of the surfaces of the rock. There are thirty thousand fossil forms of brachiopod and several types may be seen in this one localized area. Worm borings are often seen in the sedimentary rocks.

Plants have always been the basis of animal life. However, plant fossils are much less prevalent, therefore more difficult to locate. If you search very closely however, a few leaf fragments are visible in the lower regions.

Unless the ground is covered with ice and snow (a rarity in our area) collecting fossils, where not prohibited by law (collecting fossils at this locality is not permitted), can be a year-round hobby. It will take you into the backcountry where new vistas open and new friends are to be found who share this common interest. Most collect just for the fun of it and for the exhilaration of tramping in the great outdoors. There is always great excitement on the find of a perfect specimen. In the study of fossils, the rock layers open to us like a giant book, revealing the fascinating story of our own earths exciting past.

DIRECTIONS

From downtown Las Vegas, head west toward Red Rock Canyon National Conservation Area. Drive about nine miles west of Decatur Boulevard on West Charleston Blvd. Fossil Hill is on the left to the west of a new water detention basin. Fossils are found all over the foothills in this area. Remember, fossil collecting is prohibited here so simply enjoy inspecting and viewing these remnants of ancient life.

Recommended basic maps: AAA Nevada/Utah road map; Benchmark Maps Nevada Road & Recreation Atlas. Check individual topographic maps for more detailed information.

OLD ROAD
TO PAHRUMP

Winding through deep gorges, where tall ponderosa pines point their fingers skyward, climbing steep grades of gray striated rock toward a 6,700-foot summit, is the old road to Pahrump, also known as Potato Pass (or Rocky Gap). It beckons the weary traveler to explore the scenic fourteen-mile drive over the Spring Mountains. For the purposes of this chapter, the description of the route provided below assumes that the route is open for its entire length from Red Rock to Pahrump Valley. Recently, flash floods have caused closure of the section of road between Red Rock Summit and Lovell Canyon. Before embarking on this fine trip, it is advised that the desert explorer check with the rangers at Red Rock Canyon as to road conditions. If this section of road is still closed, the route can be explored from either end.

The road begins at the Willow Springs fork and ends near Highway 160, close to Pahrump Valley. In spring, cool breezes and tiny springs give way to a myriad of wildflowers, shrubs and trees along the way. Delicate orange and yellow columbine share their habitat with blue asters, star flowers and tall graceful red bells. The entire area is perfumed by the golden flowering greasewood and deep purple wild lilacs. Overhead, tall pinyons lend shade to this lovely area. Deep canyons with huge boulders perched grotesquely on the rims provide spectacular views.

Midway up the spiraling road stands a colossal pine tree. All the surrounding growth is dwarfed in comparison to this mighty giant. Its branches shelter a cleared area where picnic tables and benches have been placed. Pine needles carpet the ground and in the flanks

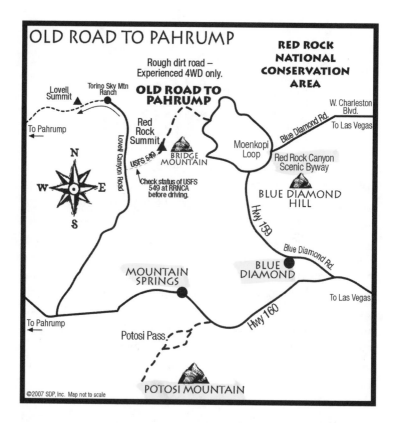

of the nearby hills small animal tracks form lacelike patterns. Gray squirrels are busy emptying pine cones for their winter hoard. Lazy lizards are content to climb upon rocks and sun themselves, while tiny field mice solemnly stare at the busy activity swirling about them. As the road continues its spiral climb upwards, hawks and sparrows may be spotted gracefully gliding on air currents high above.

The 360° views from the summit are breathtaking. Glimpses of the valley below are visible through the mouths of the deep ravines. Snow-capped Charleston Peak towers over all.

As the lazy descent into Pahrump Valley unfolds, conifers give way to yucca, Joshua and many species of cacti, a sharp contrast to the tangled forest just above. The road today is vastly different from the trail of old. The construction was under the supervision of Colonel Thomas W. Miller of the U.S. Grazing Service and labor was furnished by the nearby CCC camp personnel. This road went over the mountains to Lovell Canyon near the Roberts Ranch and Cave Springs through the Manse Ranch and down into Pahrump Valley where it ended.

The road has many hairpin turns, but its condition is good enough to give most experienced drivers a pleasant trip into this remote region. "Harrowing" can be used to describe the ride of twenty years ago.

As the seasons change, so does the scenery. The stillness of ice and snow give way to spring and the gurgling water as it seeks a pathway through the canyons and glens. Summer finds all types of animals, plants and birds readying themselves for the changing colors of fall and the long winter ahead. Prepare yourself for the most enjoyable of trips if you put this one on your agenda!

DIRECTIONS

The Old Road to Pahrump is accessed from either the south or north ends of Las Vegas. However, due to flash floods, the section now known as USFS 549 is impassable, from Red Rock Summit to Lovell Canyon. Check with RRNCA on road status prior to attempting the very rough, and sometimes closed, road to Red Rock Summit from the Red Rock Canyon side. Follow Highway 159 to the Red Rock National Conservation Area Visitor Center (paying the entrance fee). The visitor center can also be reached from the north end of Las Vegas by following Charleston Boulevard approximately 15 miles west from the Interstate. Continue on the Scenic Drive Road 7.5 miles to the White Rock Picnic Area turnoff. Turn northwest, and follow the poor dirt (four-wheel drive definitely required) five miles to Red Rock Summit (6,430 feet). At the present

The Old Road to Pahrump, impassable by vehicle due to flash floods and washouts, as seen from the air on a LVMPD Search & Rescue exercise. Photo: Wynne Benti

time, this is as far as you can go from the east. Before attemting this drive, check at the Visitor Center for updated road conditions.

Recommended basic maps: AAA Nevada/Utah road map; Benchmark Maps Nevada Road & Recreation Atlas. Check individual topographic maps for more detailed information.

RED ROCK CANYON

A few years ago only a small percentage of the residents of Nevada had visited or even passed by Red Rock Canyon. Out of state visitors were few and far between. Now, each year sees a rapidly increasing army of visitors. They come across the country to southern Nevada to explore Red Rock Canyon where nature reveals her grandest aspects.

The region once lay beneath a warm sea until it was pushed up and eroded by nature's forces, wind and rain. Today it is a maze of sun-shot hills and canyons which embody much of the mystery and contradiction of the southwestern deserts.

Red Rock Canyon is managed by the Bureau of Land Management which also maintains herds of wild horses and burros there. The visitor center is staffed by knowledgeable rangers who can answer any question on the geology, flora, fauna, and history of the canyons.

From the road, Red Rock Canyon may appear without interest to the novice desert traveler, yet seen close up it reveals beauty and hidden treasures—graceful desert willows, clear, cool remote springs, native plants, fossils, concretions, and native wildlife.

Man has created a portion of the legacy of the canyon, too. Petroglyphs that depict a group of Spanish soldiers that add to the lore of wanderings through the land. Lieutenant John C. Fremont paused with his men at a nearby spring. Even today the country is little changed. Red Rock lies under a silent and enchanted spell.

Red Rock Canyon in winter. Photo: Leslie Payne

I have long been intrigued by Red Rock Canyon. I have driven all the dirt trails and sandy washes in my Jeep and camped many years ago in the shade of the desert willows. I have hiked the colorful hills and sat silently by the crystal springs watching the activities of wild birds.

One early morning, I joined one of the staff rangers for a bird watching tour. We met at Calico Basin, a small canyon just east of Red Rock Canyon. A portion of the canyon was set aside for private homes and small ranches. Red Spring is part of the Red Rock Canyon National Conservation Area, and is a popular site for picnickers and hikers. The boulders and sandstone hills are covered with petroglyphs, which suggest that prehistoric people once farmed and camped near the spring.

From the lush green meadow we followed a barely visible trail on foot to a small pond where we spotted a Townsend's Solitaire. I am always surprised to find on these short hikes that the area is so clean and free of debris. This is the result of different Scout groups that earn merit badges doing cleanup work projects.

Continuing along the thirteen-mile paved scenic loop drive is Lost Creek Spring. This remarkable area plays host to a multitude of mountain and desert wildlife. The water coursing beneath tall, swaying conifers is a welcome sight for birds, animals, and people alike. Across the road from Lost Creek Spring is Willow Springs, a very popular picnic spot with tables, grills, tall shade trees, and many hiking trails.

Our next stop is Pine Creek Canyon. This lovely spot was privately owned in the past and farmed as late as thirty years ago. Some of the gnarled trees still bear fruit and the remains of the homestead are in plain view. To me Pine Creek is the loveliest canyon in the area. The enormous boulders that lie strewn throughout the wide, verdant canyon are the colors of peppermint sticks. The hike from the road into Pine Creek Canyon is approximately two miles and each foot of the way is filled with unforgettable sights.

Over the years, Red Rock Canyon has become known for its climbing, attracting both rock scramblers and technical rock climbers. While we were gazing in awe at the magnificent towering stone escarpment, three vehicles from Wyoming, California, and Colorado arrived carrying about a dozen young people for a weekend of climbing. One seemingly impossible climbing hill is called "Mescalito." This climb is called a "hard case climb," a self-explanatory title. Then there are bouldering climbs and one called "Peaches." Much of this climbing is done with little or no equipment except for a strong pair of hands to grasp tiny cracks in the face of the rocks, a rope and sure feet to balance on a tiny ledge. Steady nerves and plenty of intestinal fortitude are also required.

Jim Lawlor, Sr. hikes along the Black Velvet Trail. Photo: Wynne Benti

Red Rock Canyon is still a land of mystery and enchantment, a land for which the haunting melody of a flute played at dawn would be a fitting accompaniment.

DIRECTIONS

Red Rock Canyon can be accessed from either the south or north ends of Las Vegas. For the southern approach, from Interstate 15, exit on Blue Diamond Road (Highway 160) and follow Highway 160 to the Red Rock Road (Highway 159). Follow Highway 159 to the Red Rock National Conservation Area Visitor Center (paying the entrance fee). The new visitor center can also be reached from the north end of Las Vegas by following Charleston Boulevard approximately 15 miles west from the Interstate. The Red Rock Scenic Loop is 13.0 miles, one way.

Recommended basic maps: AAA Nevada/Utah road map; Benchmark Maps Nevada Road & Recreation Atlas. Check individual topographic maps for more detailed information.

OAK CREEK CANYON

Red Rock Canyon is a favorite place for hikers and picnickers in Las Vegas. However, just beyond this familiar polka-dotted basin there is an unusual adventure into Oak Creek Canyon in the foothills of the Spring Mountains.

As a tiny trail climbs, yucca, mesquite, and cactus concede their sandy desert to scrub pine, blue spruce, juniper and thick tangles of mahogany-hued manzanita. The trail ends at the mouth of the narrow canyon. As we look at the sheer perpendicular walls, a faint sound of rushing water greets our ears. This region was a popular camping ground for many nomadic and prehistoric people of southern Nevada. These Native Americans were very industrious while inhabiting this region. In the summer and the spring they busied themselves making arrows, baskets, pottery and trinkets, from material gathered within a fifty-mile radius. Oak Creek Canyon with its abundance of water and lush growth must have been one of their favorite camping grounds.

A hike to the end of the canyon, while steep and difficult in parts, is most rewarding. Clear pools of water afford green beauty while promoting the growth of wild grapevine, mountain roses and a myriad of wildflowers many months of the year. Delicate willows dip their leaves in cool pools while lacy ferns and fairy mosses form a velvety background. The tiny Calliope hummingbird is found in profusion. Truly this beauteous canyon is Mother Nature's aviary, for birds are everywhere; their trilling calls echo throughout the region. So stop, sit quietly and listen. It is a rare experience. The mountain jay's noisy call mingles with the roundelay of the song

Oak Creek Canyon Trail. Photo: Wynne Benti

sparrow, the mockingbird and the swallow.

Farther into the canyon with its ever narrowing terrain, a waterfall wafts gently down from a thirty-foot drop, deluging the terraced hillside below.

A towering pine stands at its source like a giant guarding sentinel. The flow of water attracts a large variety of animals. Bighorn sheep share the delicious water with the bobcat, fox and tiny chipmunk.

Winter brings a sparkling wonderland to this canyon. The pools are frozen to a blue glass and the waterfall hangs like a great silver icicle. Snow hushes the sound of living creatures and all is silent in this most beautiful of canyons.

DIRECTIONS

Oak Creek Canyon can be accessed from either the south or north ends of Las Vegas. For the southern approach, from Interstate 15, exit on Blue Diamond Road (Highway 160) and follow Highway 160 to the Red Rock Road (Highway 159). Follow Highway 159 to the Red Rock National Conservation Area Visitor Center (paying the entrance fee), and follow the Scenic Drive loop for 12 miles. Veer

Hydrologist Andy Zdon enjoys the solitude of a stream at Red Rock. Photo by Wynne Benti

left as the road divides. In just 300 yards is the parking area for Oak Creek Canyon. A 1.5 to 2.0-mile hike takes you to the pools and waterfall. It's a good road for any vehicle.

Recommended basic maps: AAA Nevada/Utah road map; Benchmark Maps Nevada Road & Recreation Atlas. Check individual topographic maps for more detailed information.

Florine observes a petroglyph. Photo by Leslie Payne

PAH NYAB

The wind picks up a handful of dust, and sets it down.
Faint spirals of lives, lived long ago in the desert.
j From *Dust Whorl* by Corbin

For all their splendorous serenity and their solid massiveness, the Spring Mountains west of Las Vegas can be as temperamental as a burro. The moods of the mountains shift with the wind, with the weather, with each minute and hour of the day. When these mountains go on a rampage, mere mortals can only stand by helplessly and watch in amazement.

Thundering landslides come from their towering peaks, propelled forward by flash floods consisting of huge volumes of water. Great ravines are slashed into the desert floor by these rushing onslaughts. As suddenly as it begins, it stops. For untold centuries this cycle of nature has gone on in serenity, then violence.

Pleistocene man was first to view this magnificent spectacle. The Pueblo and Basketmaker culture were next to gaze at the formidable multicolored range, but it was the early Paiute and Shoshone that dared to camp along this abysmal ravine, where they dared to tame nature's most destructive forces.

The women wove agave fiber baskets. From the center of this versatile plant they extracted the sweet mealy core and roasted it on huge mescal fire pits. Corn was planted along with beans in the loamy soil of the dunes. The older women carefully instructed the younger women in the art of root grubbing, berry picking and the harvesting of seasonal native plants.

It was also the women's task to climb into the yawning canyons and gather the highly prized pinyon nuts. This staple added much to their meager diet. The men of the tribe hunted game in the lofty mountains, dried the flesh and tanned the hides for winter use. Many traveled to remote areas in search of jasper, chert and flint. These materials were used to fashion many tools and weapons.

Darts, bird points, mescal knives, flake scrapers and projectile points were fashioned by heavy core tooling, side-strike flaking and occasionally by heat flaking. In the submontane of the range behind Pah Nyab or Mud Springs as we know it today, large outcroppings of Aztec sandstone were decorated with intricate petroglyphs.

These first American billboards told of hunting conditions, water and drought, danger and even death. Death and danger did come to the Paiute and Shoshone. Settlers arrived and greedily drove the Indians from their encampment around this life-giving spring.

The long silent canyons echoed with the sound of gunfire that finally subdued the most courageous of these Native Americans. Lush crops were trampled into dust and the clear water ran red with blood. With heavy hearts the Indians left Pah Nyab and the rainbow-hued range, never to return.

White man, unskilled in the primitive art of survival, soon learned the blistering summer sun could dry up the spring and scorch to dust the verdant crops. Summer too sent game to higher elevations where man could not venture.

Winter brought driving rain and wind, leaving the white man to freeze and starve, with supplies exhausted and his water supply as stiff as stone.

Spring found Pah Nyab deserted. The Indians who had tamed this austere region had fled and the invaders exited as though pursued by banshees.

Quiet reigned for decades. Slowly then, life began to flow into the silent canyons, for gold and silver were discovered in the nearby mountains below Potosi Mountain. Sure-footed burros led by

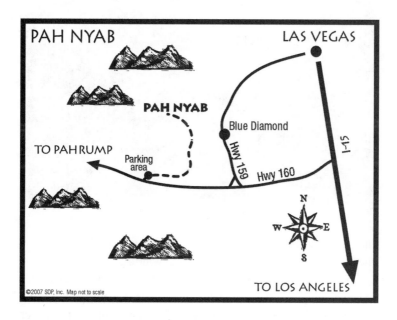

rainbow-chasing prospectors, greedily quenched their thirst at the deserted springs; sweet beans of the mesquite tree calmed the hunger pangs of man and beast alike. The silence of the ages was broken by sounds familiar to gold fields up north. Overnight camps were pitched by the steep washes. Relief from anxiety was over. Water was plentiful and a perfect night's rest assured.

With the opening of the Spanish Trail, the tranquillity of Pah Nyab was further disturbed. Heavy wagons pulled by lumbering oxen protested, with creaks and groans, each deep rut in the desert floor. While Cottonwood Spring (now Blue Diamond) was the main stop, Pah Nyab was also frequently visited by the courageous men and women who braved the dangers of the newly opened west.

Little trace remains today of Pah Nyab's fleeting populace— glittering fragments of worked chert, a deeply pitted metate, an intricately chipped arrowhead and the story of the ancient ones, told in petroglyphs on the smooth stones and walls that abound in

Upper Mud Springs. Photo: Wynne Benti

the canyon. These nomadic Indians left all of this for posterity. Of the white man, there is but a rutted trail winding into ultima Thule.

In splendorous serenity the Spring Mountains stand. Their solid mass shadows Pah Nyab, which is deserted and silent again. Racing whorls of wind that sweep across the remnants of a campfire or ancient ruins, remind us of those who lived long ago in this desert.

DIRECTIONS

The trip to Pah Nyab (called Mud Springs on the topo map) is recommended for four-wheel drive or high-clearance two-wheel vehicles only. From Las Vegas, take Interstate 15 west to Highway 160, the Blue Diamond-Pahrump Road exit. At 10.6 miles is the Blue Diamond Highway. Continue on Highway 160 (note your mileage) for about another 4.7 miles to a dirt road that heads north. Turn north on this road and follow it another 1.4 miles, where, another dirt road veers left. Go left and follow the dirt road, staying right at the fork after about 200 yards. Continue on the dirt road and at 0.6 miles, park the car and walk to the right, crossing a deep wash. Petroglyphs are scattered on all large rocks.

Recommended basic maps: AAA Nevada/Utah road map; Benchmark Maps Nevada Road & Recreation Atlas. Check individual topographic maps for more detailed information.

MULE SPRINGS CAVE

The family of scrub jays skimmed quickly across the azure sky. Something had disturbed them. The bright blue feathers of the male jay were in direct contrast to the dull blue of the female and the young ones. Except for the hurried flight of the jays, the glistening sky was as smooth as the pupil of an eye. Presently, after the jays had vanished, natural sounds returned; a woodpecker noisily drilling a hole in the decayed trunk of a mesquite; swallows singing on the high cliffs while a turtle dove moans for his mate. High on the crest of a nearby lofty hill, the mouth of a cave yawned wide to accept a group of weary Indians home from the hunt.

The windswept desert below stretched for a hundred miles or more east and west with cacti and sand its only occupants. In the old days, the word Indian brought to mind to those outside the tribal nations, an image of a painted, feather-bedecked warrior astride a racing horse chasing buffalo, as portrayed in many Hollywood westerns. Although this limited image captured the imagination of many, the Native Americans who climbed to Mule Springs Cave didn't fit this category. They had never seen a horse, lived in. a tepee, or hunted buffalo. These first Americans arrived more than ten thousand years ago, from colder northern climates.

Very different climatic conditions prevailed then. Water was more abundant as was game. We know that the prehistoric people in this area hunted camel, mastodon, the giant mammoth, and the ground sloth.

It seems almost a certainty that these early immigrants entered the North American continent via the Bering Strait from Asia. They came during the Pleistocene period, when either a land bridge existed or the strait was a frozen mass of ice. The animals are known to have crossed, and no doubt so did these ancient ancestors in pursuit of game. It seems fairly certain that this migration took place over a period as long ago as ten thousand years. This would account for the important gaps in our information about this prehistoric culture.

The prehistoric people who inhabited Mule Springs Cave had broad, heavy faces, and brown skin. Their dark hair was usually straight or wavy, and their body structure was thickset and short, with well- muscled legs from constant hill climbing.

They were the Basketmakers or Anasazi (also known as Ancestral Puebloan). Their culture was eventually to become the Early Pueblo culture of the Southwest. The Basketmakers were nomadic people following the seasons and the game. When burning winds blew across the desert, they climbed into the cool mountains, where they harvested the pinyon nut, and when the cold snows blanketed the forest floor they journeyed again to the low lands of the desert. Here they dug mescal pits where they roasted the succulent agave or century plant. The tough fiber of the yucca was used to make baskets, footwear and cordage. Arrowheads were carved from the jasper and obsidian collected on their seasonal treks. Many hours were spent carving pendants from selenite gypsum to be worn for ornamentation. They also crudely painted or etched pictures and figures into the walls of the mountains.

These pictographs and petroglyphs told of drought, of good crops or bad, of ceremonies and a host of other things. In Mule Springs Cave, the painted figures depict running men, bighorn sheep, and perhaps a lumbering ground sloth.

The floor of the cave was covered with a series of woven mats, almost two feet in thickness. It seems that when the floor became so littered with refuse, in turn making living on it almost impossible, it would merely be covered with another mat. Also found were fragments of bone, teeth, and hair of the ground sloth, arrowheads, chewing quids, lengths of cordage, many human bones, and the bones of many varieties of small animals. Potsherds were rarely located as they were heavy and cumbersome; so it seems the Anasazi primarily used the lighter baskets to carry supplies as basket fragments were found in abundance in the cave.

These tightly woven baskets could hold water, and the Anasazi cooked in them by dropping hot stones into the water. They also used baskets to cover the heads of the dead, therefore they were called Basketmakers.

Slowly the lives of the Anasazi changed. They deserted their cave dwellings in favor of houses built on the ground. In the seventh or eighth century A.D., they began making pottery. They started to grow large crops of corn, squash, and beans. Then in the 13th century the early Pueblo world began to shrink. Tree rings tell of a long and torturous drought that lasted more than twenty years.

The ancient ones drifted away, separated, or died. Little is left today to remind us of that long vanished culture. A few arrow points, a bit of cord and bones, some potsherds. Their stories are told in their petroglyphs and pictographs on the cave walls and mountainsides.

Scrub jays fly, descendants of prehistoric birds, peacefully over Mule Springs Cave now. While the lonely desert stretches across many uninhabited miles, Mule Springs Cave's yawning mouth still waits for the prehistoric hunters to return.

DIRECTIONS

This trip is suitable for four-wheel drive or high-clearance two-wheel drive vehicles only. Otherwise, anticipate hiking in from near Highway 160. From Interstate 15, take Highway 160 west to the Blue Diamond turnoff at Highway 159. From the junction, drive 14.9 miles west on Highway 160. At the Mule Springs Cave turnoff, one dirt road heads south to Sandy Valley, while the other heads north toward the cave. Turn right (north) on a dirt road. Cross under some power lines and at 0.3 miles cross a deep wash. At 0.9 miles

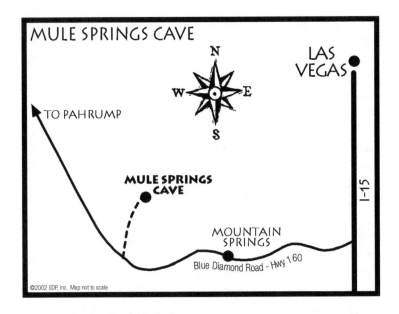

you'll see a small burned area containing some blackened yuccas (at the time of this writing). Stop the car and get out. Look to your right at the small mountain between a low mountain and a higher mountain in back. Below a rock escarpment you will see two black slots. The big slot to the right is Mule Springs Cave. Continue north on the dirt road to a fork 1.2 miles from the highway. If you park at the fork, it's a quarter-mile walk east to the foot of the hill with the cave. The left fork goes on to Mule Springs. The road is not to bad, just a few high rocks and washouts. It's okay for four-wheel drives.

Recommended basic maps: AAA Nevada/Utah road map; Benchmark Maps Nevada Road & Recreation Atlas. Check individual topographic maps for more detailed information.

POTOSI MINE

Folklore has it that "potosi" means great riches in Spanish, Aztec, or Incan. The name of the Italian saint, San Luis Potosi, was first given to a fabulous gold mine in Bolivia, to a less fabulous mine in Mexico and to any number of quite ordinary mines throughout the western hemisphere.

Indians discovered that the 8,500-foot peak, which now bears the name Potosi, contained much heavy rock. The Mormon settlers were next to investigate a report that a nearby huge mountain contained lead in vast quantities. The ore assayed out so favorably that in June of 1855, Nevada Jones dispatched men to begin the operation of Potosi Mine.

Ore smelting requires water, so a large smelting furnace was built near a spring at the base of the mountains, the first smelter ever built or operated in Nevada.

Ore was milled in large furnaces and poured into containers lined with lime. The lead was sold in great chunks all over Utah. The ore proved disappointing. It clogged the rifles when made into bullets and was shiny and brittle, instead of dull and soft, the way lead should be. With sales falling off, Indian trouble in the territory and the water supply dwindling, Jones decided to close the mine, making Potosi, Nevada's first ghost town.

In the midst of all the trouble at Potosi, an alert group of miners analyzed the lead carefully and found it contained far more silver than lead. In 1860, they formed the Colorado Mining Company and resumed operations. Log cabins were built at the site and several

Tailings at the upper Potosi Mine. Photo by Wynne Benti

stone structures housed the forty men that worked the mine. The ore proved irritatingly complex, difficult to smelt and even more difficult to separate. It contained a high content of zinc and sulphur that burned easily. After two years of hard, unproductive work, the Colorado Mining Company admitted defeat.

In 1905, the Potosi Mine was opened again. This time zinc was to play the leading role. A one-hundred ton reduction mill located in Goodsprings made it the major zinc producer in the territory. In 1913, it was the main source of zinc used in World War I. By 1926, it had produced well more than 30,000 tons of ore valued at $45,000. Again the operation did not prove economically sound and again, Potosi gasped her last breath.

Potosi Mountain, raising its head 8,500 feet in the Spring Mountain range, has viewed southern Nevada history from infancy to adulthood. Though the mineral wealth extracted from the Potosi Mine was but a drop in the bucket compared to the rest of Nevada's output, it concedes to none the eminence of being Nevada's first mine.

Today, a trip to the abandoned mine site is truly a trip into our pioneering past. Juniper trees lend a refreshing touch of greenery to the region. High on the eastern skyline is a row of window rock openings carved by erosion and wind in the layers of grey limestone. A limestone boulder weighing several tons perches atop a two-foot square pedestal.

The huge iron and wood structures on the mountainside are the remains of a roasting plant built in 1914. A climb to the mine tunnel offers spectacular views down the side of the mountain. It is hard to believe that man could have transported the massive timber and heavy equipment to these heights. The main mine tunnel is more than 1,300 feet in length. In all, there are more than four miles of underground workings. The tunnel entrance is sixty feet wide and in certain areas one hundred feet high. Near the tunnel entrance a series of steps with a cable railing has been chiseled into the mountainside.

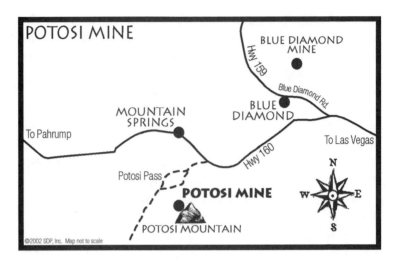

Limestone formations found all over Potosi and the surrounding canyons contain beautifully preserved fossils, remnants of the ancient warm seas that once covered the area. The breathtaking view alone is reward enough for the most dedicated hikers and adventurers.

DIRECTIONS

High-clearance two-wheel drive vehicles can get you to the base of Potosi, with careful driving over steep sandy spots. Most people will want a four-wheel drive. From Interstate 15 take the Blue Diamond exit and head north on Highway 160, 18.5 miles to the signed Potosi Mountain Road (graded dirt). Follow the dirt road 4.2 miles south to the Potosi Spring area. The road gets rough in places toward the spring. At the spring, drive up the hill a quarter mile to the Potosi Mine ruins. Some recent private property issues have cropped up, so heed all no trespassing signs.

Recommended basic maps: AAA Nevada/Utah road map; Benchmark Maps Nevada Road & Recreation Atlas. Check individual topographic maps for more detailed information.

BIRD SPRING ROCK SHELTERS

"The little minute humble though they be,
make the mighty ages of eternity."
j Carney

Desert life is stark, void of all civilization's trappings. Lovely plants that appear inviting to the touch are encased in a prickly evil smelling armor, while animals have spiny thick skins or hard shells. Men who call the desert home, whether prospector or Native American, seem all to gravitate to a common level, the grim struggle for existence.

This story is of the Bird Spring Dome area. An area typical of a desert expanse, high craggy mountains casting shadows on purple-hued mesas, while deeper canyons are void of sunlight. Thick-skinned cactus and spear-tipped yuccas grow in somber profusion on the otherwise barren hills. Man wandered into this remote territory for thousands of years.

The old Indian trail that went from seep to seep was first followed by the Anasazi (also known as the Ancestral Puebloan) or Basketmakers. Later the Paiute and Shoshone followed the lonely trail. Nights were spent in the crude rock shelters and caves of their ancestors, the Anasazi who had left many years before. Pottery was sculpted by skillful weather-worn hands, and dried by the scorching sun as hard as in the hottest kilns. Hunters spent weeks in the hills gathering pinyon nuts. The fruit of the agave was collected while strips of deer meat dried on crude bark racks.

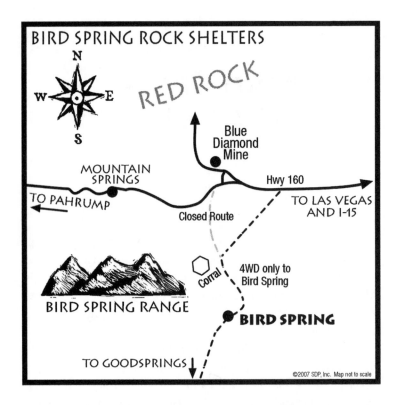

Then came the new settlers. Peace and tranquility vanished for the Native Americans. Rumbling stagecoaches invaded the quiet of the dome. Volleys of shots reverberated through the calm of the area, as the settlers drove the native peoples from their homes to make way for new communities.

The water at Bird Spring ran fifty barrels of good water a day. This alone was sufficient to make it a popular stop for stage lines, the prospector and the emigrant on their way west. This though, was a land of sizzling summer days and freezing winter nights. Food for burros and mules could only be found by men who knew the desert well. Native Americans were about the only ones who fit that category. Soon, the settlers deserted Bird Spring Dome.

The elements had won again, driving away both Native American and settler. Soon wind and rain devoured the few standing houses. Heavy boots had long ago crushed the Indian pots and bowls. Unused arrowheads and tools lay discarded around the rock shelter. Again the dome was at peace.

Now decades later, Bird Spring Dome looks as it did when the ancients lived here. Arrowheads and points may still be found on the darkened earth. These are small reminders of a culture that faded away, leaving broken bits behind. A trip into this lovely area is a trip into the pages of our past.

DIRECTIONS

This trip is recommended for high clearance two-wheel drive vehicles at least, with four-wheel drive vehicles preferred. From Las Vegas, head west from Interstate 15 on Highway 160. At about 7.6 miles, you will come to a dirt road that heads southwest in generally a straight course toward the Bird Spring area. Turn left, and follow this dirt road approximately six miles to another junction. While driving this six miles, be sure to drive carefully and rather slowly as some washouts along the road could result in serious vehicle (or bodily) damage if encountered at too high a rate of speed. Turn left on the dirt road, continuing up to Bird Spring. You will pass two old corrals near a small spring.

Recommended basic maps: AAA Nevada/Utah road map; Benchmark Maps Nevada Road & Recreation Atlas. Check USGS topographic maps for more detailed information.

*A canoe trip down the Colorado River from Willow Beach is a great way
to see Queho's Cave. Photo: Wynne Benti*

ALONG THE COLORADO RIVER

PETE HARDIN'S LOST MINE

Deep in the Eldorado Mountains south of Boulder City, six to eight miles south of Eldorado Canyon, on the old road to Callville, is a lost mine. It's not just another lost mine colored by legends and stories passed down through generations of burro men. It's an authentic lost mine discovered about fifty years ago. On the receiving end of this tale of gold was a dear friend of mine, noted author and miner, Charles Labbe.

The tale goes as follows. Prospecting was well into its final death gasp around 1909, yet there still lingered some tried and true diehards. Old Pete Hardin was one of these. At a spry eighty years of age, he had not yet given up hope of finding "the really big one." Rumors had led him to the foothills of the McCullough Mountains in search of the Lost Mormon Diggings and to the lofty Panamints after Breyfogle's Lost Ledge. The mysterious Avawatz Mountains had all but claimed his life as he searched for the Lost Burro Mine. He had combed the Funerals seeking Adams' Lost Ridge, and mighty Tucki Mountain for whatever treasure to be found there. All of his searching was futile. Old Pete was persistent, though. Maybe, just maybe, his fortune would be found on the next grubstaked trip.

Summer is dead hot in the Eldorado Mountains. The black igneous rock retains heat like the furnaces of Hell. On one particular trip into the foreboding place, it seemed to Pete that the face of the entire mountain had changed. A landslide, perhaps? A cloudburst? Where was the known spring? He should have arrived at its cooling waters an hour ago. Forlorn Hope Spring seemed to be worthy of its name on that hot July day.

PETE HARDIN'S LOST MINE

LAS VEGAS

LAKE MEAD

HENDERSON

HOOVER DAM

BOULDER CITY

Colorado River

WILLOW BEACH

Queho's Cave

LOST MINE

NELSON

TO KINGMAN, ARIZONA

HWY 95

160

Eldorado Canyon

TO SEARCHLIGHT

LAKE MOHAVE

©2007 SDP, Inc. Map not to scale

Nevada is a state rich in minerals, so freaks of fortune are inevitable. Mines are often discovered by accident and the stories told about them are a mixture of fact and fantasy. A vital part of western lore, these stories are really what the west is all about.

Creosote bushes offer scant protection from the summer sun for man or beast and on this particular day both Pete and a four-foot long rattlesnake sought its meager shade. Although 80 years had dimmed his eyesight a bit, Pete was still a good shot. A bullet hit the target and the second one split a rock in half, revealing a vein of pure gold.

Was it the end of the rainbow at last for old Pete? He began a close examination of the surrounding territory and when daylight faded he lay down to sleep, an elated and rich man. Many footsore and weary days passed until Pete stumbled into the small mining camp of Buckskin, just outside of Searchlight, Nevada. He showed his find to three men, one being Charles Labbe. Pete excitedly rambled on about "gold that just littered the ground." Morning found

At the foot of the Eldorado Mountains. Photo: Wynne Benti

Pete laden with supplies, a burro, and a promise to return and share his fortune with his friends.

That blistering July day was the last time anyone ever set eyes on Pete Hardin. When he didn't show up at Buckskin, a search party was sent out to find Pete and his gold. Forlorn Hope Spring and the entire area revealed nothing. The gold is surely still there. Somewhere, too, are Old Pete's bones. Both are waiting to be discovered.

DIRECTIONS

From Las Vegas drive east toward Boulder City to the junction of Highways 93 and 95. Drive 10 miles south on Highway 95 to the Nelson exit (Highway 165), and continue past Nelson. Dirt trails take you into the Eldorado Mountains. Camping in the El Dorado Mountains is primitive and all minimum impact camping methods should be observed. For further information, contact the Bureau of Land Management office in Las Vegas.

Recommended basic maps: AAA Nevada/Utah and Colorado River Area road maps; Benchmark Maps Nevada Road & Recreation Atlas. Check topographic maps for more detailed information.

Burro-driven arrastre used for crushing ore at near Nelson. Photo: Leslie Payne

ELDORADO, NELSON, AND SEARCHLIGHT

In the late 1800's, Eldorado was Nevada's largest port on the Colorado River, with an estimated population of 1,500. Wood-burning steamers performed miracles on the shallow, muddied upriver trip from Arizona. Sometimes they had to resort to backing up over the sand bars, letting the powerful blades of the ferry boats churn a passage, then turn and steam through.

Mining was at its peak in 1863, so a ten-stamp mill was built to process the ore from the Techatticup Mine, the Gettysburg Mine, and the Savage Mine. At the turn of the century, the town of Searchlight boomed, and soon Nelson was built at the head of Eldorado Canyon.

The history of this area would not be complete without mentioning the notorious Paiute Indian renegade, Queho. His story has been told and retold for years. After murdering two men in the Eldorado District in December 1910, he fled on foot, but because he had one leg shorter than the other, his footprints were distinctive. The posse tracked him to the Arizona side of the river where a third victim was found. However, there was no trace of Queho.

Early in January of 1919, the sheriff's office in Las Vegas was notified of two more murders and a set of limping footprints at the scene. On January 21, 1919, a Nelson resident was shot and killed and the well-known tracks were again in evidence. But Queho wasn't to be located until 1940 when his mummified body was found in a high cave in the side of Black Canyon. The discovery of Queho was the biggest media event the area had seen since the building of Hoover Dam. Photographers came from as far away as New York to get a shot of Queho.

The cemetery at Nelson. Photo: Wynne Benti

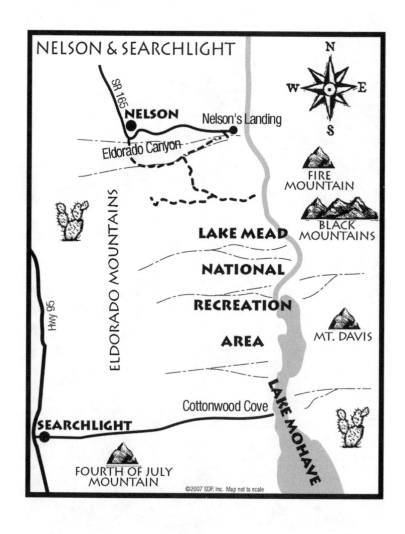

NELSON & SEARCHLIGHT

SR 165

NELSON

Nelson's Landing

Eldorado Canyon

ELDORADO MOUNTAINS

Hwy 95

FIRE MOUNTAIN

BLACK MOUNTAINS

LAKE MEAD

NATIONAL

RECREATION

AREA

MT. DAVIS

Cottonwood Cove

LAKE MOHAVE

SEARCHLIGHT

FOURTH OF JULY MOUNTAIN

©2007 SDP, Inc. Map not to scale

The glory days of mining in Eldorado and Nelson faded long ago. Nelson caters mostly to fishermen who drive down the canyon seeking trout or bass spots on the Colorado. Some visitors come just to see Nelson while a few prospectors comb the hills for treasure. The possibilities are endless for camping, hiking, exploring, and fishing in this northern end of Lake Mead National Recreation Area.

At the junction of Highway 95 and State Route 164 is Searchlight. The first mining claim here was located by G.F. Colton in 1895. Legend has it that his partner told him:

"If you want to find gold in that claim, you'll need a searchlight."

But Colton had the last laugh. The mine produced more than $6,000,000 worth of ore.

The most famous mines in the Searchlight area were the Duplex, Pompeii, Blossom, Cyrus Noble, Quartette, and Good Hope. Most of the mines encountered water at a depth of three hundred feet and many of them had their own mills.

In 1907, the Santa Fe Railroad built a spur line that connected Searchlight and another small hamlet called Barnwell, with the railroad's main line. Unfortunately, diminishing profits, duplicate service at Nipton on the Union Pacific Railroad, and the coming popularity of automobiles caused the railroad to cease operation. It was dismantled in 1929.

Searchlight hasn't changed much from the early years. Mine structures are still in evidence. Many of the old houses still stand, sagging a little more with each windstorm. The residents are friendly and love to talk about the "old days."

Although Searchlight doesn't have any regularly scheduled events, there is great bass fishing at Cottonwood Cove, just east on Route 164. There are several cafes that boast of real home cooking. The area surrounding Searchlight is lovely for exploring in spring or fall. There are many places to camp, both near Searchlight and along the river. This is a colorful region of Nevada's past.

Old miner's cabin in the Eldorado Mountains. Photo: Leslie Payne

DIRECTIONS

From Las Vegas take Highway 95 south 10.0 miles to State Route 165 and turn east. Nelson is approximately 12.0 miles south on 165 which can be followed to its end at Nelson's Landing on the Colorado River. Searchlight is located at the junction of Highway 95 and State Route 164, about 36.0 miles south of Highway 93. Cottonwood Cove, on Lake Mohave, is directly east of Searchlight at the end of State Route 164.

Recommended basic maps: AAA Nevada/Utah and Colorado River Area road maps; Benchmark Maps Nevada Road & Recreation Atlas. Check individual topographic maps for more detailed information.

PECTOLITE NEAR BOULDER CITY

If you are one who likes to wander the far reaches of the desert searching for rocks, some very interesting specimens can be found only a short distance from Boulder City, Nevada, on the shores of a very accessible dry lake. Pectolite, an unusual mineral, was brought to my attention several years ago by an old prospector who told me these specimens were little fossilized teeth of prehistoric animals.

The pectolite specimens held out for my inspection were pretty. Some were fibrous crystals and soft; others were quite hard. One that had been polished caught the light with the effect of a white cat's eye. He said the supply was abundant and scattered over a wide area.

There was also another reason for visiting this same dry lake. For years, I had heard mention of an odd crustacean which resembled something between a trilobite and a seagoing roach in fiesta costume, which appeared in the pools of water on the lake bed, following a good rain. Friends of mine returned from the lake bed and told me about these creatures with yellow, red and blue markings, but the thing sounded so fantastic I could hardly believe it. A trip to the library did not turn up the identity of the creatures, nor did a visit to a school biology teacher.

We returned to the lake after seasonal rains had left standing pools and found some of the aquatic curiosities swimming around. Using a reference book, we finally were able to find a description of a similar type of crustacean that lived deep in the mud and hibernated until enough water collected on the surface and then came up to reproduce.

Several trips after goodly rains have failed to lead to any more of the creatures to photograph, and if I had not seen them myself I would think of the search for them as being like a snipe hunt from childhood days.

The hunt for pectolite, though, is never disappointing. A fine selection of specimens is washed out by every rain and their glowing whiteness against the brown lake bottom makes them easy to collect. I can also understand how they could be mistaken for fossilized teeth. Most of these minerals are found in radiating groups of tiny fibrous crystals. Some of them are hard, but we have found fancy groups with fan designs and sunbursts of fiber that are much harder.

Pectolite is one of the minerals found in association with the zeolite minerals, but differs from this group in that it has no aluminum in its formula. It is a calcium sodium silicate. Some of the harder pieces make lovely gems when polished, with a silky quality that is quite pleasing to look at.

Pectolite is supposed to occur most commonly in volcanic trap rocks, and this locality is no exception. Even on the shore of this dry lake, so far from their source, evidence is plentiful that it occurred in cavities of igneous rocks along with, and sometimes inside of, chalcedony geodes. Small bits of chalcedony abound in this field. Some of them have pectolite still attached. These and the small quartz crystals found in the float are indications of a wonderful field back in the hills just waiting to be explored.

It appears that these pectolite specimens and chalcedony fragments have weathered out of the hills in back of the lake. The terrain in that direction is rough and so far I haven't heard of anyone who has tried to locate the source. One of these days, someone will travel up the alluvial fan and make the discovery. In the meantime, there are plenty of pectolite specimens for those interested enough to drive to this intriguing dry lake near Boulder City.

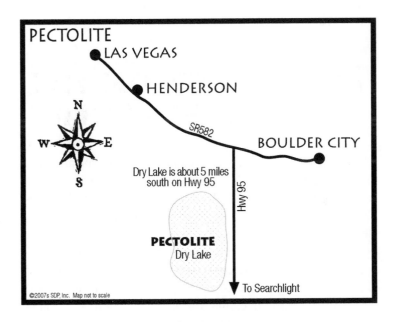

DIRECTIONS

From Las Vegas, drive east toward Boulder City, then take Highway 95 south toward Searchlight. Drive 6.8 miles to the rim of a large dry lake which is plainly visible. Search the edges of the lake. Collecting is best after recent rains.

Recommended basic maps: AAA Nevada/Utah road map; Benchmark Maps Nevada Road & Recreation Atlas. Check individual topographic maps for more detailed information.

TWO PLACES ON THE COLORADO RIVER

Just outside of Las Vegas, the Colorado offers her splendors in a more accessible manner than anywhere else along the river. There are spectacular hikes through fractured cliffs and chiseled washes. Those who hike to the lofty mesa tops are rewarded with panoramic views of the river. It gleams below them like a ribbon of liquid silver as it snakes its way past hidden coves and small sandy beaches. Fishermen, boaters, photographers, artists, outdoorsmen and picnickers all find a special secluded paradise in this surprising area.

Across Hoover Dam on the Arizona side of the river is Willow Beach. Its marina is a mecca for water people. Ducks paddle lazily around the small harbors gathering in large noisy groups when offered popcorn, bread or crackers.

In the not too distant past there was once a popular restaurant, hotel, and store, however Willow Beach sits at the bottom of a large desert wash, which follows the road you drive in on to get down to the marina. The desert's natural history is one of thunderstorms and unexpected flash floods. Willow Beach is no exception and during the past fifteen years has been subjected to several major flash floods, one of which washed out several buildings and parked cars.

According to some locals, the hotel was closed by the park service because the didn't want anyone staying there when a flash flood hit. The question of safety still looms large. At the time of this writing there was a store and as the proprietor explained, they signed a large liability waiver to operate it. Parking is for a limited time and those who do leave their vehicles in any wash along the Colorado River, do so at their own risk.

Enjoying Boy Scout Hot Spring on the Colorado River below Hoover Dam.
Photo: Wynne Benti

Ringbolt Rapids. Photo: Florine Lawlor Collection

The current is so slow on this portion of the Colorado River that it is enjoyable to canoe down to Lake Mohave and back with an overnight camp in one of the canyons (on high ground) along the way.

Moving slowly around the hairpin bend back toward the dam, you enter a different world. In early morning all is silence save for the muffled gurgle of the river's voice and the keening cries of cormorants as they circle high above. Every now and then one will stiffen and plunge like an arrow into the glistening surface of the water. After a few rings of ripples disappear into nothing, the bird will suddenly catapult upward, a flash of metallic silver in its beak signaling the mission's success.

The river changes at every moment. Places of mild turbulence are next to deep pools where fish seem to hang suspended in a block of lucite plastic. So clear is the water that you can see gills open and close and observe the movement of the fins.

On one side there may be cliffs more than a hundred feet high, while on the other bank is a miniature enchanted cove. Sometimes in one of these oases of sand and willow, a herd of bighorn sheep can be seen. If you are quiet, they may remain quite unafraid, but if startled all you will see is a glimpse of their white heart-shaped backsides as they bound gracefully away.

Finally, you will arrive at Ringbolt Rapids. More than 100 years ago, large iron rings were anchored into the towering canyon walls at Ringbolt. Cables were then threaded through the rings so riverboats could winch themselves over the churning rapids. Unless you have a powerful engine on your boat, this will be as far as it is possible to go. In a dizzying swirl of current you can turn and head back to Willow Beach. If coming by canoe or raft from the base of Hoover Dam, you can zip right through the rapids from above.

There are three hot springs in Black Canyon between Hoover Dam and Willow Beach. All three can be reached by canoe from the put-in point just below the dam via a car shuttle to the marina.

The river can be followed a short distance past the marina in the opposite direction. If you beach your boat in any number of sandy coves along the eastern bank, remains of ancient Indian campsites may be observed. Pottery sherds and chert chips attest to the fact that the ancient people sought to be near the nurturing river.

Ringbolt Rapids can also be reached by hiking, although the walk is long, tiring and should only be attempted by very experienced desert hikers. Do not hike this route during the summer or on hot days due to the increased risk of heat-related illness and flash floods. Carry plenty of water, Gatorade, or a packet of electrolyte replacement to add to your water.

The scenery is spectacular. Following the tortured convolutions of a gravel wash, the route takes the traveler into a narrow passage hewn through the looming cliffs by past floods. First on one side, then on the other, canyons of lacy greenery beckon stretching fingers that point to the very heart of the mountains. The silence is complete.

When it seems that this primeval world has swallowed you up forever, the craggy cliffs widen into a large level beach at the river's edge. On the opposite wall can be seen the large rusted rings once so important to navigators on the Colorado.

As you face the river to your left, approximately one mile along a steep trail is a natural hot springs called Arizona Hot Spring, known to river runners as "Ringbolt." There is welcome shade under the trees and soothing relaxation in the thermal pond. Don't get too limp. It's a long hike back up to the car.

DIRECTIONS
WILLOW BEACH

Take Highway 93 from Las Vegas through Boulder City to the Alan Bible Visitor Center at Lake Mead National Recreation Area for information on the entire area. Willow Beach is approximately 22 miles from the Visitor Center on paved highway. The turnoff to Willow Beach is signed.

RINGBOLT RAPID AND ARIZONA HOT SPRING

Take Highway 93 from Las Vegas through Boulder City to the Alan Bible Visitor Center at Lake Mead Recreation Area. Seven miles from the Visitor Center turn left onto a dirt parking area. Follow the path downhill under the road. The gravel wash leads to the river. Only experienced desert hikers should attempt this and not during the summer or on hot days due to the increased risk of heat-related illness. Carry at least two quarts of water or Gatorade.

The hot spring is located near the rapid onshore, and requires a twenty-foot climb up some permanent rings. There are two other hot springs of note on the river above Arizona Hot Spring—Sauna Cave and Boy Scout. The best way to reach them is by canoe or raft down Black Canyon. The launch point for Black Canyon is just below Hoover Dam, with the take out point at Willow Beach Marina.

Recommended basic maps: AAA Colorado River Area, Nevada/Utah, and Arizona/New Mexico road maps; DeLorme Nevada and Arizona Atlas & Gazetteer. Check individual topographic maps for more detailed information.

GYPSUM CAVE

Through every rift of discovery some seeming anomaly drops out of the darkness, and falls, as an important link, into the great chain of order in our universe. Still munching the succulent spears of the fibrous yucca, the ponderous ground sloth made his way into the cool depths of a large cave. The summer heat had lingered late that year and the cave offered shelter from the burning sun, not only for the now extinct sloth, but also for Pleistocene man.

Deep in the limestone spur of the Frenchman Mountains where the cave is located, a slight tremor began reaching quake proportions only seconds later. Masses of loose rock and shale plummeted from the cave's domed ceiling crushing animal and man alike. Tons of limestone and selenite gypsum partially blocked the vast entrance to the cave leaving the dark interior to be undisturbed for what was to be countless centuries.

In the spring of 1924, Dr. Mark Raymond Harrington had his first inkling of the cave. Several old-time Nevadans told him of the legends that surrounded a large gypsum cave in the rugged Frenchman Mountains. Some of these old-timers claimed that a band of renegade Apaches had hidden out there while the unsuspecting lawmen rode within throwing distance of their quarry. Tales were also told of tangled dried seaweed that carpeted the entire floor of the cave. Still, other stories about the eerie cavern placed a taboo upon the entire neighborhood.

Dr. Harrington, however, was only spurred on by these strange and mysterious tales. Forming an archeological expedition, he decided to explore Gypsum Cave for himself. In 1925, he and his party made their way into the low entrance of the fabled cave and from there to its depths. It was here that Dr. Harrington found one of our most important links to the golden chain of the past. In this cave he found that man and beast had lived contemporaneously in the Southwest more than 8,000 years ago. This underground labyrinth had entombed knowledge that was to discredit all earlier claims of man's first existence in this area of southern Nevada.

Gypsum Cave received its name from the huge deposits of selenite gypsum that make up most of room number four. The entrance to the cavern is sixty-five feet across and more than fifteen feet high. It drops sharply in the first fifty feet, then abruptly levels off. The slope is extremely hazardous due to the rock slides that affect this area from time to time.

The cave is divided into five sections or rooms, measuring a total of 300 feet. The widest spot reaches over one hundred and twenty feet and the narrowest but seven feet. Most of the rooms lie below the level of the mouth.

In room number one, just southwest of the cave's opening, there is a series of crevices that house a great number of small black bats. This room was occupied more frequently by man than any other portion of the cavern. A layer of refuse measuring over twenty inches in depth is the prime indication. The first layer consisted of ash, charcoal, burned sticks, chert, flint chips, bones, numerous shells of the desert tortoise as well as pendants fashioned from the ever present gypsum. There are braided cord, small potsherds and metates or grinding slabs. This layer told of frequent visitors and of the early Pueblos who seemed to have remained for the longest time. These industrious people fashioned the clear-cut crystals into pendants for ornaments to barter with other tribes. The Basketmakers frequented the cool deep cave. They hunted the prized bighorns that sought refuge in the cavern.

Layer two consisted mainly of dung, worked gypsum, cordage, and atlatl darts. Layers three and four were very much the same. It was in the fifth and sixth layers, that evidence of the herbaceous

A geologist at Gypsum Cave. A fence around the site protects it from vandalism. Photo: Leslie Payne

ground sloth and Pleistocene man was discovered.

In one place, abundant sloth hair was found only inches from a chert knife, indicating that man had hunted the huge beast. Room number three contained brightly painted dart fragments along with gaming sticks, stone choppers and scrapers. Flints of a black obsidian were located near the surface with a broken flint knife and two pieces of sinew string.

When the electrical system cuts out in the middle of nowhere,
it's handy to be traveling with friends. Photo: Wynne Benti

In room five, many specimens of great interest, both archeological and paleontological, were uncovered. An entire sloth skull and a beautifully shaped dart point fashioned of white quartzite with the sealing wax still on it greatly excited the diggers. Coarse hair also indicated the Tanupalama camel once used the cave for shelter. A few pieces of decorated pottery were unearthed near a prominent fire pit. One of the most interesting finds was a hollow deer hoof rattle that no doubt had been used in some ceremonial rite.

At the northwest end of the same room, the large wing bone, and feather quills of a giant California condor were found, near the intact skeleton of a newborn sloth and that of a species of a small, now extinct horse.

In looking over the interesting collection of artifacts found in Gypsum Cave, now on display at the Southwest Museum at Highland Park, California, the question of food stands out as of

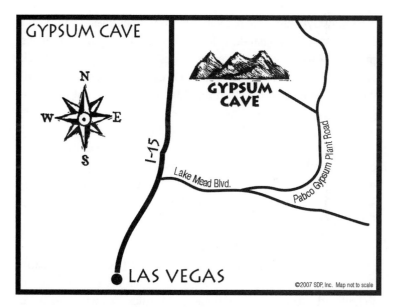

utmost importance. In room number one, which was inhabited by prehistoric man, many bones of food animals remained. Evidence of vegetal foods was also prevalent.

The bighorn sheep and the rabbit seem to have had top priority as favorite meats while corn, four types of cultivated beans, and the sweet screwbean from the mesquite held first place as a side dish. Among other wild plants in evidence were the agave and aloe.

Going beyond the study of the inhabitants of the cave and their implements, we find the cave was formed during a very wet period of ancient history; this in turn was followed by increasing dryness terminating in the extreme arid condition we find today.

Research shows that the last extremely wet condition in this part of our state was at the time of the great glacial activity during the Pleistocene period. If this is true, then the strata of the cave would indicate that the culture in the lowest level of the cave (sloth and man) would be 10,500 years of age, or from about 8,500 B.C.

Today Gypsum Cave has suffered from thoughtless visitors and is surrounded by chainlink fence. However, overall it remains much as it was those long centuries past. The ceiling is still black with the soot from long extinguished fires, the opaque gypsum still glows when a torch is held near. Huge rocks still lay at the same grotesque angles as they first did some 8,000 years ago when a shattering earthquake caused them to crash to the ground.

True, an attempt has been made by man to discover the links to our remarkable past in the vast interior of this cavern, but he has disturbed little. The cave itself remains as it was, high on a limestone spur in the Frenchman Mountains, or Sunrise Mountains as they are now more commonly called.

DIRECTIONS

Take Interstate 15 north to Lake Mead Blvd. (North Shore Road). Turn east and drive 11.2 miles until you reach the Pabco Gypsum Plant Road. Turn left and continue for 2.9 miles. You will cross three washes. A small dirt road leads west to the base of a mountain and a walking trail continues up the mountain for 400 feet to the cave that is highly visible from the road at 2.4 miles. The road is paved until the trail, though the gravel is rough.

As with all of Florine's trips, when she first visited the Gypsum Cave, the area around it, from the North Shore Road all along the Pabco Gypsum Plant Road, was a pristine remote backcountry experience. Sadly, as Las Vegas has expanded this area has experienced its share of illegal littering and dumping. We kept this trip in the book because of its archaeological significance, but we urge all visitors to treat all of Nevada with care and respect.

Recommended basic maps: AAA Colorado River Area and Nevada/Utah road maps; Benchmark Maps Nevada Road & Recreation Atlas. Check individual topographic maps for more detailed information.

BUFFINGTON POCKETS

Webster's Dictionary defines a pocket as a hollow, enclosed place. This description is a rather drab uninspiring definition for a most colorful and unusual site. In the early 1920's a cattleman by the name of Warren Buffington wandered into this small bit of paradise and enthusiastically claimed it to be the prettiest acreage he'd ever set foot on. The burnt oranges and reds of the sandstone were in bright contrast to the water that flowed freely from a spring in a narrow twisting canyon just south of his pocket. The walls of the canyon were decorated with early petroglyphs of the nomadic Indians who frequented this area many years ago.

In the cliff walls above his newly-built cabin were shallow caves that once sheltered these same prehistoric Indians. Sage, squaw-bush, and a great variety of prolific desert plants provided ample desert forage for cattle, and thus both man and beast thrived. In the years spent at his pocket, Buffington erected a large cement wall at the head of the canyon to catch the spring water as well as the rain water and so assured himself of cool water the year around.

On the west side of the small valley a quarry was opened and soon the air resounded with the boom of explosives and machinery as they cut the great slabs of Aztec sandstone from the hillsides. The pink veined stone resembled marble but unfortunately proved to be too soft for most needs and the quarry eventually closed. Next to appear on the scene was a mine of white silica. It too operated for a while then work there also was discontinued. Buffington boarded up his cabin and moved on, restless like most men of his breed, leaving only his name as a reminder that he once lived here.

Warren Buffington's water reservoir. Photo: Wynne Benti

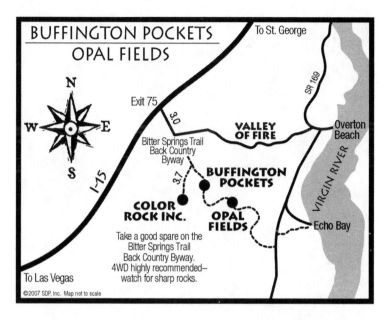

Today, Buffington Pockets is still a small bit of paradise verdant with heavy growth, nestled in the varicolored sandstone canyon as serene and quiet as it was centuries ago. The water lies in deep pools reflecting the unusual petroglyphs on the smooth cliff face. It is a beautiful spot for picture-taking. The hills are easily climbed and who knows what treasures may be found in the small narrow Indian canyons that abound in this region. A more enjoyable spot would be hard to find!

DIRECTIONS

Drive east on Interstate 15 to the first Valley of Fire exit (Exit 75 - plainly marked). Turn right and drive approximately 3.4 miles to where the road bends to the left. Continue straight 4.2 miles on the dirt road heading toward the Muddy Mountains (Bitter Springs Trail) to a fork. Follow the signs toward Buffington Pockets. Petroglyphs can be found behind the reservoir up the wash. Suitable for high clearance two-wheel drive vehicles though four-wheel

Another view of Buffington Pockets. Photo: Andy Zdon

drive is recommended. Make sure you have a good spare tire, as the limestone cobbles in the road can be rough on a set of tires.

Recommended basic maps: AAA Colorado River Area and Nevada/Utah road maps; Benchmark Maps Nevada Road & Recreation Atlas. Check individual topographic maps for more detailed information.

OPAL FIELDS

In this rocky flat below Muddy Peak, and just a stone's throw from the Valley of Fire, is a real adventure for the rock collector, professional or amateur alike. Many wonderful days have been spent poking around this wonderful area.

Chalcedony, which is the waxy form of quartz, is lying in profusion, over a vast area. The larger rocks, when cracked open, house a variety of colored agate, banded in shades of red and pink. Onyx is black, white and brown. White variegate is prevalent, as is carnelian or sard.

Some of the nodules are opalized and look as if they had been carefully polished and cemented into the gray limestone. The true opal, which is a non-crystalline form of white pearly quartz is scattered somewhat sparsely among the other trivia. The common opal in the region is pale yellow to brick red and is quite translucent and resinous.

Much of the quartz material or chalcedony that is common in this area is usually of volcanic origin; some of the more highly colored pieces are prized as gemstones by the collector. Also on this same flat table, perhaps centuries ago, primitive man gathered the flint jasper and hornstone that were widely used for the making of tools. Wide evidence of conchoidal fractured chips have been found throughout the valley.

If time allows, search the nearby hills for some unusual fossils. A wormlike structure neatly divided into segments can be found on a sharp gray outcropping. Large pieces of tabulate coral and sponge can also be found. Our most extraordinary find was a caryocrinites or cystoid, an extinct marine animal of the Cambrian period.

The road past the opal field winds on toward Lake Mead and passes through rugged volcanic mountains pitted with gaping holes and caves. The vegetation is surprisingly dense with a wild and colorful array of desert blooms. At the end of this rutted dirt road, Echo Bay looms into view, a wet welcome sight at the end of a most rewarding tour.

DIRECTIONS

After passing cabins at Buffington Pockets, continue for exactly three miles. At the highest point on the road, turn right to opal fields, about 0.1 miles. Suitable for high clearance two-wheel drive vehicles. Four-wheel drive is recommended.

Recommended basic maps: AAA Colorado River Area and Nevada/Utah road maps; Benchmark Maps Nevada Road & Recreation Atlas. Check individual topographic maps for more detailed information.

MESA HOUSE
LOST CITY MUSEUM, OVERTON, NEVADA

Summer showers had given the verdant scrub growth a soft glow. The great mountain forests and lush meadows hung heavy with mist, while lazy streams made their way toward the journey's end, a sylvan pond. Was this the Garden of Eden? No, this was southern Nevada 20,000 years ago. It was at this time that man first discovered the area. He came to hunt the giant ground sloth, elk, camel, and the other native animals that once roamed this territory. Few skeletal remains have been found of these ancient people, although wide evidence of their craft has been excavated and studied. They were skillful at chipping flint and chert for spears, darts, and atlatl throwers. They tanned hides for clothing and wove crude shoes from the fiber of the agave or century plant.

Slowly the climate began to change. The streams became mere trickles. The ponds evaporated, affording the most meager liquid to animal and man. Few species survived this devastating drought. The forests fell and became stone. Plants withered and blew away. Man and animal moved on or died.

Into this new arid land came the Pueblo culture, a nomadic people. They wandered in search of game and water. This migration eventually took them into the Moapa Valley area where they left a treasure house of archaeological remains.

The first report of Pueblo cultural remains was submitted by Jedediah Smith when in 1827 he revealed his "find" to William Clark. In this report, he said that he had unearthed an unusual pipe and a large intricately chipped chert knife in a cave of salt near the

Mesa House reconstruction

Virgin River. A late expedition into the valley discovered mines of salt worked by the Indians. Nearby, there appeared to be the ruins of an ancient city. It was not until 1900 that archaeologists reported wide evidence of early Indian settlers. Mescal pits, pottery, stone tools, and charred bones were located in abundance. In 1924, John and Fay Perkins of Overton began extensive exploration of this lost city. By 1925, Nevada Governor Scrugham had contacted the Heye Foundation in New York. They sent a research party headed by Dr. Mark Harrington and began the excavation of the Moapa Valley "Mesa House," "Lost City," and "Casa Grande."

One of the most fascinating ruins was that of the Mesa House. This 85-room dwelling was built during the last period of the Puebloan occupation in southern Nevada. Situated on a large mesa more than 150 feet above the valley floor, it commanded an awe-inspiring view in all directions. This unhampered vista provided an excellent defense for the inhabitants.

The main feature was a central courtyard intersected with many narrow entrances. Pit houses and other aground structures encircled the courtyard. Located nearby were the remains of many fire pits.

The fertile valley floor was cultivated. Squash, corn, and a peculiar type of melon were grown and dried for winter use. Domestic

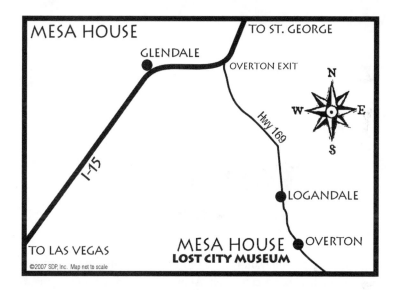

MESA HOUSE

TO ST. GEORGE

GLENDALE

OVERTON EXIT

N

W — ⊙ — E

Hwy 169

S

I-15

LOGANDALE

TO LAS VEGAS

MESA HOUSE
LOST CITY MUSEUM

OVERTON

©2007 SDP, Inc. Map not to scale

plants along with wild foods provided ample supply for the entire population.

About 1150 A.D., Mesa House and all surrounding settlements were abandoned. The reason for their disappearance is not clear though there has been much speculation on the subject. Perhaps a lingering drought, a plague, or potential raids by other groups were the cause. There is no evidence of violence or fire in the ruins.

During the archaeological excavation, 289 burials were uncovered. Decorated pottery was usually found along side the body and in certain instances tools and ornaments were placed nearby.

DIRECTIONS

A reconstruction of Mesa House as well as fascinating exhibits regarding Mesa House can be seen at the Lost City Museum of Archaeology in Overton. From Las Vegas take Interstate 15 north and to Exit 93. Drive south from Exit 93 through Logandale to Overton. The museum is located on the west side of the highway. Call ahead for hours. *Editor's note: Mesa House as described in earlier editions of this book was obliterated by off-road vehicle use and development. Visiting the former site of Mesa House is no longer recommended.*

Recommended basic maps: AAA Colorado River Area and Nevada/Utah road maps; Benchmark Maps Nevada Road & Recreation Atlas. Check individual topo maps for more detailed information.

TOLTEC GOD
IN NEVADA

The Moapa Valley, northeast of Las Vegas, holds many mysteries and guards her secrets well. Above the valley, on a wide mesa, are the remains of an extensive civilization called "Pueblo Grande de Nevada," the largest Anasazi settlement in Nevada. Very little is known of the people that settled here, where they came from, or where they went when they deserted the plateau so suddenly. Some students of early history say a plague wiped them out. Others theorize that a long drought forced their exodus. Some don't even try to speculate.

Skeletal remains of these early inhabitants were found inside round structure foundations located on the mesa. The strange burials give testimony to their existence, as does the fact that the ground is covered with bits of pottery. Rare incised stones, rock shelters containing fossilized bones of the prehistoric ground sloth, hand-hewn stone tools, delicate projectile points, primitive sandals woven of agave and yucca fiber have also been found in Moapa Valley. Pots and cooking vessels number in the hundreds. Much of the material discovered has been dated and attributed to a specific tribal group. There is one piece, however, which remains an unsolved and tantalizing mystery.

Early in 1927, an old Southern Paiute man, who wandered the valley searching for bits and pieces of anything useful, made an astonishing find. He discovered a replica of the great god Tlaloc, revered rain deity of the Toltecs, tucked away on a protected ledge in the mesa. How and why was this small carved stone statue brought thousands of miles from Mexico to Nevada's Moapa Valley? How long had it laid in the sheltered place so strange and so remote from its own ancient realm? What was the real significance of its solitary presence in southwestern America's mysterious cradle of vanished people? Was there a connection between the small god and the people of the mesa?

It had been placed carefully in the deep recess of a natural rock bench overhung by a massive protective boulder. Evidently, it had lain for centuries in undisturbed security until the elder found it. As to the queries, none live to answer and the stone oracle cannot speak, but in its make up is a clue to its origin.

The idol was carved from a hard, carboniferous limestone that corresponds to the rock in the country of the Toltecs. The limestone in the Moapa Valley, where it was discovered, is very different. Logically, the inference is that the figure may have been wrought in the desert valley where it was first brought to light. Perhaps through an inexorable decree of fate an individual or group of people was transplanted from the distant Toltec domain to the harsh, arid environment. They brought the little rain god with them, placing it in the small cave when came the hour of departure for eternity. Was there a relationship between the Toltecs and Paiutes of Moapa Valley in the long distant past that would account for the strange little figure? Yet, that theory leaves unsolved the strangeness of material used. Perhaps Moapa Valley contains a similar and yet undiscovered deposit. All of this opens a fascinating field for speculation. Sphinx-like is the riddle of Tlaloc, a victim of amazing isolation.

Three-quarters of a century has passed and no ultimate developments have ever taken place. The small, silent god is as forgotten as the cave in which it was found. I have the unqualified word of an archaeologist (who prefers to remain anonymous) that the man who lifted the idol out of its dusty niche on the rock shelf made one of the most remarkable discoveries in America. Many may have passed by the figure without seeing it, in its coating of fine silt driven in by desert winds and caked by the slight moisture that infrequently penetrated the rock fissures. The sharp eyes of the old man, however, told him there was something artificially placed and his inherent curiosity led him to investigate.

The archaeologist referenced to on these pages, is thoroughly conversant through direct field contact with principal discoveries in the sphere of the Toltecs and Aztecs in South America and in our own southwest. He is therefore qualified to pass judgement on and identify the figure plucked from the cleft it had occupied with unchanging serenity through the passing of untold ages.

The image is in a sitting position with its small legs (of which there is only a suggestion) drawn up. Elbows rest on knees and the chin is cupped in the palms of its hands. Its total height is four inches. The head measured 1.875 inches from front to back and one to two inches from side to side. The eyes are large and set well apart, the nose well formed and the mouth wide and expressive.

The work reveals a surprising grasp of art on the part of the sculptor. The features and posture are that of profound meditation. There is no semblance of distortion so often prevalent in this type of work. Though in an excellent state of preservation at the time of its discovery, the limestone god was pitted, the ravages of time that defies imagination to encompass, since its span is estimated at 4,000 to 8,000 years. Also, the tiny object was quite heavy.

Finding the idol did not greatly interest the old man. He was more interested in its value and the price he might get for it. Discovering that it contained neither gold nor silver, he at first tossed it aside. Then, he remembered a man who collected such things and retrieved it. He kept the figure until his next trip to Bishop, California, where the man lived. The Bishop resident, a collector of most everything, purchased the Toltec carving from the old man. Through a chain of most unusual circumstances, the collector had come to possess a piece anyone would revere.

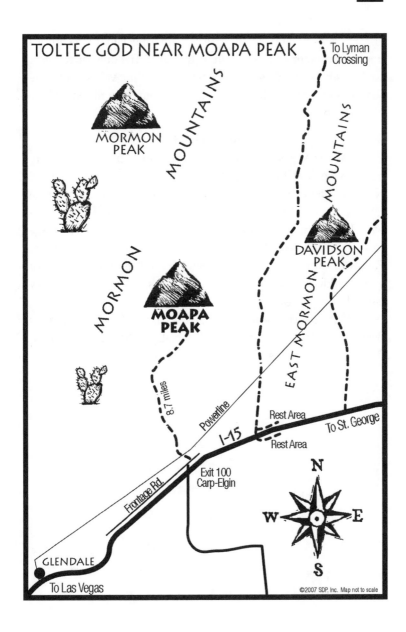

TOLTEC GOD NEAR MOAPA PEAK

To Lyman Crossing

MORMON MOUNTAINS

MORMON PEAK

EAST MORMON MOUNTAINS

DAVIDSON PEAK

MORMON

MOAPA PEAK

8.7 miles

Powerline

I-15

Rest Area

To St. George

Rest Area

Frontage Rd.

Exit 100
Carp-Elgin

N
W E
S

GLENDALE

To Las Vegas

©2007 SDP, Inc. Map not to scale

The cave where the tiny carved figurine laid for centuries might hold other secrets. Where is the cave? The only directions I could resurrect are these: a long, narrow, winding valley under the shadow of the mesas. Maybe I'll meet you out there this fall. I'll be looking too.

DIRECTIONS

From Las Vegas, take Interstate 15 north approximately sixty miles to Exit 100, the Carp/Elgin exit, seven miles past Glendale, Nevada. After exiting at the truck parking area, follow the frontage road back along the interstate to where it crosses under the highway. Follow the road under the freeway, then right on the frontage road about 100 yards to a junction with a dirt road heading north. Follow the dirt road 8.7 miles, passing a corral and power lines to a good parking area. The road ends in a small protected valley beneath Moapa Peak.

Recommended basic maps: AAA Nevada/Utah road map; Benchmark Maps Nevada Road & Recreation Atlas. Check individual topographic maps for more detailed information.

SALT MINES OF THE ANCIENTS

Over the high mesas and across the barren mountains, winds a deep path carved by water. When I first visited the Salt Mines almost 30 years ago, one word dominated all of my thoughts as we drove into the shadowy recesses of the wash leading to the Salt Mines of the Ancients—unexplored!

This little known region lies within a few feet of the Colorado River and only a short distance from the Valley of Fire. A dusty, winding road leading from North Shore Road has made the salt mines fairly accessible in the past, but recent high water levels in Lake Mead have inundated this site.

The country is a wild tumbled maze of arroyos, bluffs, and deep washes so rough and rugged that it is rarely explored by man. From the edges of the sheer walls that confine the washes one can scan a land so void and silent it is almost uncanny in its solitude. Here the earth is fractured by a series of jagged cracks running in every direction. The mountains in the background have been chiseled, gouged, and carved by wind and water.

When the lake level drops enough, small crystals of salt give sparkling evidence of the nearby ancient mine. Salt and gypsum are precipitated from salt lakes that are subject to excessive evaporation. At this salt mine, both gypsum and salt deposits were found in great abundance just above the silt floor of the long dry lake. Stratified layers of salt indicated multicolored impurities, but a crystalline blue cast was evident.

In the center of the sixty-foot wide salt deposit was a broad fissure or crack that seemed to lead into the very core of the mountain. On

Salt mines of the ancients above water. Photo: Leslie Payne

either side of the fissure, deep pits were evidence of the ancient miners' industry. We have very little knowledge of these peoples' way of life. We can only assume they used salt much as we do today; as a flavoring, a preservative, or possibly its main use in ancient times could have been for barter. On the mesas above, a network of trails lead to small chipping areas where a variety of chert, jasper, and flint may be found. Peculiar patterns are formed by a series of rocks placed carefully by human hands for a purpose unknown today.

The Anasazi vanished a long time ago, but the land where they once lived is just as it always was — barren, desolate, and brimming with beauty.

DIRECTIONS

From Las Vegas take Interstate 15 north, then south on Highway 169 following signs to Overton Beach in Lake Mead National Recreation Area (approximately 24 miles).

With the expansion and increasing popularity of Lake Mead National Recreation area, there is a marina, visitor's center and ranger's

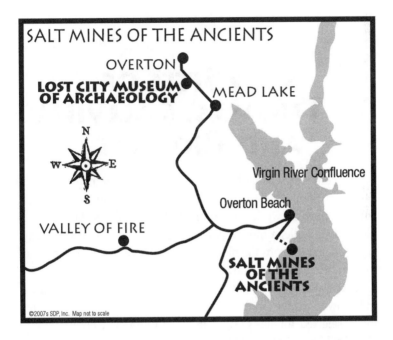

headquarters at Overton Beach. A locked gate has been installed across the wash leading down to the Salt Mines which have been submerged for several years by the waters of Lake Mead. The rangers at the visitor center say that the only way to get to the site is by boat, or long day hike. Nevertheless, Overton Beach makes a wonderful day trip. Enjoy a picnic in the pleasant surroundings while imagining what this place was like during the days of the salt mines, or even thirty years ago when Florine first came here.

Recommended basic maps: AAA Nevada/Utah and Colorado River Area road maps; Benchmark Maps Nevada Road & Recreation Atlas. Check individual topographic maps for more detailed information.

OLD SITES OF ST. THOMAS, CALLVILLE, AND RIOVILLE

Human eyes will probably never again see the many historic sites now under the waters of Lake Mead. Rioville, brought into being by the hard work of the Mormon pioneer, Daniel Bonelli, and old Fort Callville, a monument to Brigham Young's vision, today lay drowned beneath the blue waters of the vast lake now behind the concrete barrier of Hoover Dam.

Fort Callville, originally known as Call's Landing, lay about a mile downstream from the mouth of Hoover Canyon, the site originally selected for the great dam, which although built in Black Canyon, bore the name of Boulder Dam for many years until it was renamed for late President Hoover. Callville marked the headwaters of navigation on the Colorado. When the water was high enough, stern wheel steamboats brought cargo and passengers who transferred from ocean going ships on the Gulf of California.

Brigham Young wanted the town of Callville to serve as the Mormon port to the sea. They could export their products and import needed goods without having to transport them across California or the eastern states. They would only have to haul a short distance by wagon instead of across the plains on one side and over the Sierra Nevada on the other.

A group of dedicated men under the leadership of Bishop Anson Call founded the settlement in December of 1864. Within a few months, a substantial stone building about one hundred and twenty feet long by thirty feet wide had been constructed. Seventy-five feet was occupied by a warehouse to hold the expected mer-

Abandoned cars near the townsite of St. Thomas during a period of low water on Lake Mead.
Photograph from the collection of the James R. Dickinson Library, University of Nevada, Las Vegas

chandise. The rest was a store and living quarters. The ruins of this and other stone buildings in the vicinity, were still clearly visible when the lake closed over them. They showed a settlement that was quite extensive, and covered several acres.

Some twenty miles upriver from Callville was Rioville, a cluster of stone, adobe, and log houses at the mouth of the Virgin River. Around 1865, Brigham Young sent Daniel Bonelli to establish a farming community along the banks of the Muddy River, with the purpose of growing cotton. In the Moapa Valley of southern Nevada, he broke away from the colony and established a ranch and a ferry that crossed the Colorado River at the mouth of the Virgin River.

Bonelli's greatest accomplishment was the founding of Rioville, a green and fruitful little paradise in the midst of the desert. The flat lands at the junction of the two streams were cleared of mesquite thickets, leveled, and irrigated with water brought down in ditches from wing dams built on the banks of the Virgin some distance above the ranch. A fruit orchard and cottonwood trees for shade were planted and a herd of cattle flourished as did a flock of poultry.

The ranch house was Bonelli's pride and joy. It was a large stone structure on a terrace overlooking the Colorado River on the Nevada side just above the mouth of the Virgin. Along the east and south sides ran a high porch formed by an extension of the roof and supported by wooden posts. Inside were six good-sized rooms, five with fireplaces. There was a large storeroom running back into the hill against which the house was built. The roof was supported by heavy hand-hewn beams concealed from below by painted canvas tacked on to form the ceilings. Upon the beams lay planks and upon these was spread adobe clay, extra thick, as a protection against summer's blistering heat.

Other buildings furnished quarters for ranch hands and visitors, along with the usual granary, storeroom, blacksmith shop, and gristmill powered by burros. There were several corrals. The Paiute ranch hands had a camp of their own a short way up the Virgin River.

In its prime, the little Rioville settlement was a place of importance. The main road from Kingman, Arizona to Panaca and Pioche in Nevada, and to St. George and other southern Utah points crossed the Bonelli Ferry. Consequently the traffic of wagons, travelers on horseback and afoot was considerable and business was good.

Bonelli also ran a post office and did a large business in hay and grain, which he raised on the ranch and sold to the mining camps then operating in the vicinity including Chloride, White Hills, Eldorado Canyon, Mineral Park and Gold Basin. He also sold beef to the camps and the rock salt he mined on a claim seven miles distant. The traveler could buy staple groceries and such luxuries as chickens, butter, and eggs at the Bonelli store.

Rioville became just another ghost town after Bonelli died in 1904. His children moved away. The mining camps shut down and traffic along the road was diverted elsewhere. Irrigation dams washed out during a flood and no more water came to nourish

OLD SITES OF ST. THOMAS, CALLVILLE, AND RIOVILLE

TO I-15

N
W   E
S

LOGANDALE

Virgin River

OVERTON

LOST CITY MUSEUM OF ARCHAEOLOGY

MEAD LAKE

Virgin River Confluence

SITE OF ST. THOMAS

Overton Beach

VALLEY OF FIRE

LAKE MEAD

NATIONAL

RECREATION

AREA

TO THE SITES OF
RIOVILLE
(AKA JUNCTION CITY)
CALLVILLE

Echo Bay

©2007 SDP, Inc. Map not to scale

Ruins of St. Thomas today. Photo: Wynne Benti

Bonelli's little paradise. Orchard and shade trees perished. The ferry boat rotted. The road connecting Rioville with St. Thomas and the outside world was washed away. Finally, nothing remained but a group of ruined buildings. On a high gravel point behind the ranch house was the lonely grave of the man who had planned and created it all.

Occasionally when the waters of Lake Mead are low due to a dry year or two, the ruins of Callville, St. Thomas, and Rioville will reappear. Now, for the most part, they sleep in a watery bed and sightseers of today who sail across the lake never realize the historical drama that lies beneath the blue waters.

DIRECTIONS

From Las Vegas take Interstate 15 north to the Overton exit (Highway 169). Drive about eleven miles south to the Lost City Museum where you can find out more information about the lost cities of St. Thomas, Rioville, and Callville, underwater. During rare times of low water, the old foundations can be seen.

Recommended basic maps: AAA Colorado River Area and Nevada/Utah road maps; Benchmark Maps Nevada Road & Recreation Atlas. Check individual topographic maps for more detailed information.

DEVIL'S THROAT

Mysterious happenings often occur in the lonely desert. Some are explainable, and some are not. One such occurrence is the "Devil's Throat" or "Bud's Hole" as the old timers in the area call it.

The level, sandy floor of the desert seems to have been swallowed deep down into the bowels of the earth, leaving only a cavernous pit not visible until one is almost upon it. The lip of the huge, bowl-shaped depression is crumbly and soft, so beware of standing too close.

There have been many explanations as to the cause of this phenomenon. Some believe a huge meteor was responsible. Others claim it is the core of an extinct volcano. With every new visitor, there is a new theory.

As one stands near the edge, the imagination runs wild. What kind of prehistoric happenings caused the earth to collapse and sink into the devil's domain? The surrounding environs present an eerie picture. Silence seems to close in around you only to be broken by a muffled cracking sound from the pit below. Animals and plants have apparently forsaken the locality for more pleasant surroundings.

There is a simple explanation for the Devil's Throat. The most accepted theory maintains that the hole was formed when the water table rose, soaking a large deposit of gypsum, which then collapsed upon itself creating the massive cavern. With each subsequent rainfall the gypsum crumbles slightly, dissolves and sinks into the ground. As the years pass, this process of erosion takes its toll on the depression.

World renown geologist and caver, Mark Stock, sizes up Devil's Throat before dropping over the edge. Photo: Andy Zdon

The true explanation is very simple, but confidentially I prefer to think a giant prehistoric pterodactyl once nested there. What do you think?

DIRECTIONS

From Las Vegas, drive Interstate 15 north about 70 miles and exit at the Riverside/Bunkerville off ramp (Exit 112). Drive three miles passing the site of Riverside and crossing the Virgin River to the Gold Butte Road (a Bureau of Land Management Back Country Byway). Follow the Gold Butte Road south about 20 miles to some fine Aztec Sandstone outcropping marking Whitney Pockets. Stay right and continue another 9.3 miles to a fork. Turn west, heading back to Lake Mead National Recreation Area. Devil's Throat is marked.

Recommended basic maps: AAA Nevada/Utah road map; Benchmark Maps Nevada Road & Recreation Atlas. Check individual topographic maps for more detailed information.

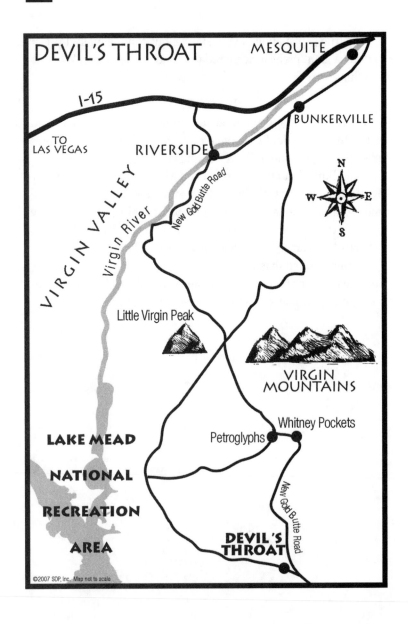

DEVIL'S THROAT

MESQUITE

I-15

BUNKERVILLE

TO
LAS VEGAS

RIVERSIDE

New Gold Butte Road

VIRGIN VALLEY

Virgin River

Little Virgin Peak

VIRGIN
MOUNTAINS

Whitney Pockets

Petroglyphs

LAKE MEAD

NATIONAL

RECREATION

AREA

DEVIL'S
THROAT

New Gold Butte Road

©2007 SDP, Inc. Map not to scale

SOUTH OF LAS VEGAS

GOODSPRINGS

Gold! Silver! Platinum! These are the rare and precious minerals that have lured prospectors and miners to distant and inaccessible places. From steep and craggy mountains to arid sandy deserts they have searched, always with one thought in mind. Is it just beyond the next bend?

For those who came to Goodsprings and the surrounding area, hope became a reality, for here they found a veritable bonanza, with cool, clear water and rich, precious ores. Water has always played an important role in mining, and where water was pure and abundant, the mining camps flourished.

Thus did Goodsprings grow. In 1886, Mormon miners from Utah built the first houses. Many others followed in rapid succession. In a very short period Goodsprings took on all the aspects of a full-fledged boomtown.

The Yellow Pine was the largest of all the mines and therefore supported most of the town's population. Gold was the richest and most predominate ore in the workings, but there were also many other minerals extracted from the deep shafts. Lead and zinc were represented in all classes. In this district there were also many copper deposits, however, none were as rich as the lead and zinc.

Today, the mine dumps still contain brightly colored ore. At the Monte Carlo Mine there is an abundance of pure white smithsonite. The Christmas Mine contains fluorescent calcite while at the Lincoln and Bill Nye mines, vanadium crystals are profuse. More than forty types of fossils have been located and identified in the surrounding mountains. The Red Cloud and Copper Chief mines are rich in cinnabar and cobalt, as are several other nearby claims.

In its heyday, there were twenty-five producing mines in the area. The Keystone Mine was credited with being the oldest. Some mines are still being worked, so if you visit the area, please respect the "No Trespassing" signs.

To the north of Goodsprings, near the Potosi Mountains, an old rock formation can be explored. It is made up of stratified sandstone overlain by limestone. At one time this laminated red and yellow rock was quarried and sold as flagstone, but because of its softness and tendency to crumble, all work soon ceased in the quarry.

A visit to the town of Goodsprings, named for the early prospector Joseph Good, is a trip into the past. Many of the original homes and buildings remain unchanged. In fact, very little has changed since the town's boom days.

Although the lovely old hotel burned to the ground quite a few years ago, most of the timeless landmarks still stand. The post office deserves special attention as does the entire area of this once famed Nevada mining town.

Past the mines and toward the middle of the "loop" lies Sandy Valley, formerly called Ripley. During the Goodsprings boom, Sandy was publicized as a real estate "find." Wagon loads of speculators were brought in from Los Angeles two or three times a week to look over the land and to view the town plot maps. It was a real estate spectacle that assumed the atmosphere of a carnival. The show ended abruptly with a thud that echoed for many months. The only building of any size still standing is the Sandy Mill, a broken-down remnant of past glory days.

Today, Sandy Valley is experiencing a resurgence. Population is growing rapidly, not because of rich ores, but because of those who seek to get away from the rush of city living. Old and new, deserted or booming, a trip to Goodsprings and Sandy Valley is an extraordinary one, even for those who prefer to see the sights from their car window.

Shafts in the Goodsprings mining district along USFS 507. Photo: Wynne Benti

DIRECTIONS

From Las Vegas, drive south on Interstate 15 south to Jean, Nevada. Then follow State Route 161 west a little over six miles to a fork. Stay right and continue a half mile to Goodsprings. To reach Sandy Valley, one can return to the fork and continue on Route 161, crossing a pass, and dropping into Sandy Valley. An alternate route to Sandy Valley, is to head northwest on the well-graded dirt road, crossing Wilson Pass (5,023'), and dropping southwest into Sandy Valley. The desert explorer can use both routes to form a fascinating loop trip.

Recommended basic maps: AAA Nevada/Utah, California, and San Bernardino County road maps; Benchmark Maps Nevada and California Road & Recreation Atlases. Check individual topographic maps for more detailed information.

LOST DIAMONDS OF THE McCULLOUGH RANGE

The McCullough Mountains are steeped in mystery. Tales told by desert dwellers and wanderers have been embellished and changed until fact is difficult to separate from fiction. An old desert man who lived in Nelson between the Colorado River and the McCullough Mountains told me this tale, but swore me to secrecy.

"We've got to search it out," he would say. "When I'm gone, then you can write about it, if it's still there . . . that is, if I haven't found it."

Well, my dear friend is gone now, so I'll tell you his story.

Shortly after World War I, prosperity was at a peak and tales of adventure gripped the world. It was at this time, when three men rented a small plane and flew to Las Vegas to buy many thousands of dollars worth of diamonds. They landed in the morning at what was then Alamo Airport and left the plane to be refueled. They went into town to make their purchase and to try their luck at a casino before heading back to Los Angeles.

Las Vegas weather in April is quite unpredictable. It can be bright and sunny one moment, cloudy and rainy the next. This long ago April day was no exception. A clear sky in the morning turned to slate gray by mid-afternoon with more than a hint of rain in the air. The pilot and his two passengers returned to the airport about 4:00 p.m. and hurriedly took off for Los Angeles. Minutes after they were in the air the rain started falling in torrents and the pilot, inexperienced in such conditions, flew off course. Another small plane headed for Las Vegas spotted them over the McCullough Mountains.

Rain iced on the wings of the plane. The pilot panicked and ordered all excess luggage, seats, and gear to be thrown overboard. In their terror, even the small metal case containing the unmounted diamonds was mistakenly hurled into the growing darkness. Luck was with them as the storm lifted. The winds subsided and the small plane headed swiftly toward Los Angeles with the three still frightened men.

They made a successful and uneventful landing in Los Angeles; uneventful that is, until they started groping around for the small diamond container. With sinking hearts they realized they had thrown it out over the mountains near Las Vegas, $50,000 worth of diamonds—a fortune. All the money they had was invested in those sparkling gems. Now their money and treasure had been tossed to the wind.

They were stunned. What could they do? Wait! The mountains hadn't seemed that high or lengthy. They could form a search party and find the box of gems. So with spirits heightened again, they planned a return trip.

Returning to Las Vegas the next day, they asked about the terrain and the mountains they had flown over. They were told that the mountains were called the McCullough Mountains and contrary to their analysis, the mountains were quite high and very lengthy. Undaunted, they rented a vehicle the next weekend and went to Nevada with the town of Nelson as their destination. After talking with a few of the locals, they found a resident who knew the terrain as well as he knew his own backyard. He agreed to take them on their search for the diamonds.

They began their journey. Hours passed into days, days into weeks, and by July the weather was so hot they had to call a halt until fall. The wait was agonizing. Blistering heat stretched endlessly through August and September. Finally, by the middle of October they resumed their quest.

By March they were so discouraged, they agreed that the mountains had won. The diamonds were gone, swallowed up by the wilderness. Reluctantly, the three friends left Nevada, knowing that it was futile to search any longer.

The McCullough Mountains abound in stories of phantom treasures but those who knew about the diamonds swore each other to secrecy. My friend never told a soul. He continued to search for many years, but his search, too, was fruitless.

I have pondered over the fate of those ice-blue gems. Did the box fall into one of the many deep mine shafts that dot the hillsides? Did the case break on impact and scatter the stones? Why wasn't the case, their luggage, or for that matter, any of the airplane seats ever found? Perhaps it wasn't the McCullough Mountains they flew over, although all clues point in that direction. Could the case of diamonds have fallen into a crevice, onto a tree top, or even into the Colorado River? Has someone already found the diamonds and kept quiet? At any rate, it is a true story and is worth an occasional treasure hunt. Perhaps someday the mystery will be solved.

DIRECTIONS

The McCullough Mountains stretch north and south from Henderson past Jean, Nevada. You can drive into them on any dirt road. This is rough, remote country. Four-wheel drive is required to navigate over poor dirt roads where any roads exist at all. Be prepared for plenty of hiking. When you venture into remote desert areas take plenty of water, a full tank of gas, a spare tire or two, tools and a cell phone. Tell a friend where you are going and when you plan to return.

Recommended basic maps: AAA Nevada/Utah, California, and San Bernardino County road maps; Benchmark Maps Nevada and California Road & Recreation Atlases. Check individual topographic maps for more detailed information.

Two Turquoise Treasures

CRESCENT PEAK TURQUOISE

Azure blue like a summer sky, yet as deep green as the churning sea, this describes the turquoise deposit found by Indian Johnny in 1894. The mine held some of the finest turquoise the west had ever seen. The stones were highly prized by most southwestern Native American nations as ceremonial gems, and increasing popularity as a commercial jewelry item made the find a valuable one.

Comprised mainly of hydrous phosphate of aluminum, turquoise receives its delicate coloring from the small amount of copper it contains. When completely dry, the stone has a tendency to fade and lose some of its color and depth. When the stone retains its vivid hue, its wearer is said to be charmed.

The stone was also thought to have great healing powers and was used extensively by tribal shamans to restore good health. It adorned tribal dress in many ways and was carried by hunters as a good fortune amulet.

Indian Johnny was running cattle near Crescent Peak when his sensitive ears picked up the faint wail of a terrified calf. Urging his horse onto a full gallop, he came upon the unfortunate animal wedged in a narrow crevice. With much effort he succeeded in freeing the hapless calf. As he rested after the tiring struggle, he noticed stones lying about his feet had an opaque blue cast. Chipping away the rough outer crust, Johnny found himself looking at a vein of the finest turquoise he had ever seen. The rocky crevice contained enough of the precious gemstone to provide a generous supply for many years to come.

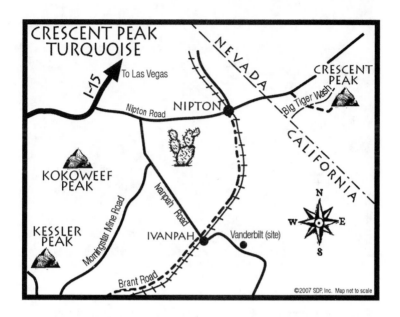

Crescent Peak was soon a beehive of activity. Indian craftspeople carefully extracted the gleaming stones from the black submontane just as their ancestors had done for some 10,000 years. The stones were sorted and rubbed to a luster, then cut into a variety of sizes, some so small that a pine nut shell could hold a dozen. They were then drilled and sewed to soft deerskin clothing and moccasins. Some of the larger stones were fashioned into necklaces. These beautiful objects never cease to amaze contemporary jewelers, as only the most primitive tools were used in their manufacture.

In 1905, a second cry of "GOLD!" echoed throughout the west. Claims sprang up at an alarming rate. Within months, claim markers with the unlikely names of Nipper, Bugnet, Blue Star, Fino, and many more, were recorded. In August 1905, a post office was opened and until July 1908, it handled a large amount of mail. Following the opening of the post office, the first mill opened. Two ceremonies were a fitting achievement for this booming camp. It was a rich strike, or so it seemed.

Hiking Clark Mountain. Photo: Wynne Benti

Veins of gold, twist and drift, and sometimes disappear completely. So it was with Crescent Peak. The once busy camp became quiet. Wind and rain demolished the frail structures. Sand and rocks covered the pitted hillsides. After five years of activity and eighty years of solitude, this area is again as close as it will ever be to prehistoric times, before the first miner attacked the earth with crude stone tools. The soft dirt at the base of the mountain holds many secrets in the form of a stone chipping knife, a primitive scraper, perhaps a bead or two or a rusted gold pan. These are the remnants of an eon of mining.

DIRECTIONS

From Las Vegas drive south on Interstate 15, crossing the state line into California. Exit at Nipton Road. Head east on Nipton Road, passing through the town of Niption, then cross back into Nevada. Turning south on a graded dirt road approximately 14.8 miles from the interstate. The road crosses Big Tiger Wash, and heads generally east toward Crescent Peak. There are still private property holdings out here so observe and respect all posted signs.

CLARK MOUNTAIN TURQUOISE

The second turquoise area is in the Clark Mountain Range of southern Nevada. For centuries men have searched her deep canyons and lofty heights for riches. Gold and silver worth millions of dollars were taken out of the old Ivanpah mines in the late 1800's. Indians found turquoise in saucer-like depressions. Prospectors dug deep shafts and tunnels looking for copper and lead. Spanish explorers reportedly cached treasure worth a king's ransom in the foothills. One story even tells of Mayan Indians leaving intricately carved turquoise fetishes in a hidden cave deep within the Clarks.

Today the mountain still guards her secrets. Few have explored the remote, twisting, dark canyons where a motherlode of turquoise is said to be. Although collecting the turquoise is strictly prohibited here, the lure of seeing the beautiful blue mineral in-situ drives the explorer onward. On our last trip to these mysterious mountains, we were tracking down a new clue to the turquoise treasure that had recently come to light. As we entered the vast upper reaches of Clark Mountain, we left the truck and climbed the rugged terrain on foot. High winds made progress slow.

After climbing for several hours, we spotted what looked like the remains of a camp: tumbled shacks, twisted bits of leather and rope, battered cooking utensils, and the inevitable rusty cans and broken glass.

Making a hasty search for anything that might provide a clue, we found the date "1873" carved deeply into a half-buried wooden post. Noticing a faint trail leading into a narrow canyon, we hiked until shadows began to darken the walls. We camped the night and after a light breakfast the next morning we sighted the mouth of a cave some eighty feet above us. Scrambling up the rugged slope, I found a bottle deeply purpled by the sun, two old frying pans, a coffee pot, several tent pegs, a small gold watch chain and, half covered in the soft dirt, a bottle filled with turquoise nuggets! Here at last was the indication we had been seeking that the fabled treasure was near.

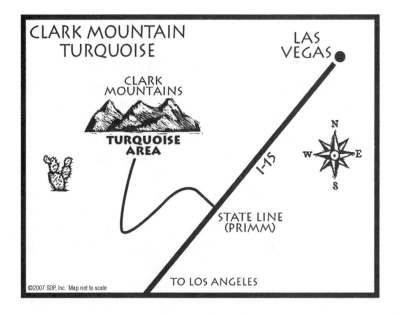

CLARK MOUNTAIN
TURQUOISE

LAS
VEGAS

CLARK
MOUNTAINS

TURQUOISE
AREA

N

W — E

S

I-15

STATE LINE
(PRIMM)

©2007 SDP, Inc. Map not to scale

TO LOS ANGELES

We explored the terrain around the cave for two more days, without success. We knew we were on the right track. The fabled cache of turquoise was somewhere nearby, so we made plans to return, perhaps in the winter when the brush is not as thick as in springtime. Maybe we will be able to locate a marker or some other obscure clues we missed before.

INFORMATION

Gas, food and lodging can be found at State Line (Primm). The roads into mountains are fair to very poor dirt. Four-wheel drive is recommended.

DIRECTIONS

From Las Vegas take Interstate 15 south to State Line, about 54 miles. From Whiskey Pete's Casino, follow a dirt road southwest past an old cattle pen at 3.1 miles. Continue on for 4.2 miles to reach the turquoise area in the Clark Mountains.

Recommended basic maps: AAA Nevada/Utah, California, and San Bernardino County road maps; Benchmark Maps Nevada and California Road & Recreation Atlases.. Check individual topographic maps for more detailed information.

MASHBIRD'S LOST MINE

GOLD! In all ages the curse of humankind. To gain it, men yield honor, action and lasting renown, and for it, barter their very souls.

Have you ever read stories of lost mines and treasures? Have you been obsessed with the notion of finding a lost or hidden cache? Do they seem out of reach like the elusive end of a rainbow?

Having just put down such a book, we gazed at the line of hills visible from our front yard. The colors seemed to change from the bluest of blues to the brightest of gold. For in any of these shadowed canyons on its rugged sides, the Lost Mormon Mine may someday be found, while we grow obsessed with the desire to search for lost bonanzas.

First, a great deal of time must be spent in research. Clues must be followed and directions noted, until we are sure we can pinpoint the region. All available information is before us.

Dutch Mashbird approached the sunned surface of the sandstone cliff. Carefully he scanned the outline of the mountains, his mind recording every unusual detail. He was very anxious that there would be no mistaking this area when he returned after filing his claim. He painstakingly sketched a map and wrote in his precise script a complete description of the newly located gold claim, carefully depicting the drift of the lode, the hardness of the ground and the quality of the combined hornblende-silver and gold ore. The sandstone grew cold before he finished his legendary chronicle.

Folding the paper meticulously, he concealed it inside his shirt. His partner, who had quietly observed Mashbird all that long day, was the last man to see the map and descriptive text, for Dutch

Mashbird was ruthlessly assaulted down the road to Las Vegas Ranch and left for dead. His partner was struck a blow on the back of his head that was to prove fatal.

Mashbird recovered consciousness, though his skull was fractured. Not realizing the seriousness of his condition, he stumbled on, determined to reach the assayer's office and file that claim. Hours passed and the pain in his head became increasingly worse. He felt dizzy and his memory was blurred. He finally fell to his knees, doubled with the pain. It was like this that a group of Native Americans found him. They treated his wounds, fed him, and nursed him back to health, though he was never to completely recover his senses.

Dutch Mashbird, still weak and confused, made it back to the makeshift camp where he buried his map and chronicle, never to find it again. He rambled on from story to story, from camp to camp, and from one grubstake to another, always searching, never finding. Until his death, Mashbird searched.

The map remains where he buried it. The gold remains where he found it, and Dutch Mashbird lies in a nameless grave, all of his secrets buried with him.

We began our search, competing with that legendary burro man who, when he was alive, knew every inch of the somber McCullough Mountains. We decided to acquire a modern burro called a dune buggy that had the agility of a mountain goat and the dependability of a burro. Loaded with picks, gold pans, water and food, we headed for the hills. Fifteen or twenty miles northwest of Searchlight, Nevada we found a spring of clear water. It was there that we made our camp. Leaving all roads and the camp behind, we climbed gradually, and entered the brown undulating folds of the McCullough Mountains. Faint wagon traces were visible at scattered points, a mute reminder of wagons long since gone.

Several times, we happened upon old mining camps with antiquated household wares. Silvered wooden shacks braced themselves against the next windstorm. Still, no sign of the long abandoned camp of Dutch Mashbird. We wondered if we would be the first intruders into that deserted dwelling—that is if we found it at all.

Our search will go on as others have before, for the drive in a person that pushes he or she toward a golden cache will never be halted, slowed down perhaps, but never halted. If this trip proves fruitless, we shall try again. Perhaps it will be you who will beat us to old Dutch's lost mine?

DIRECTIONS

Access to the McCullough Range can be most conveniently obtained by using the following route. Remember, this is a lost treasure that could be anywhere in the McCulloughs. From Las Vegas, drive south on Interstate 15 to the Nipton Road heading toward Searchlight. Drive 18.1 miles east on the Nipton Road, to a dirt road on the north side of the road. Head north on the power line road 3.9 miles to a junction and turn west on a rougher dirt road. Follow this dirt road 3.7 miles (staying right at a fork en route) and park. Four-wheel drive is recommended for this route.

Another rougher route heads toward the McCulloughs from State Line. Drive east past the Primadonna Casino. In 0.2 miles, continue east on a graded dirt road and follow it 0.8 miles to where it meets a power line road. Drive the dusty power line road two miles, crossing some railroad tracks en route to a broad fork. Head right and drive 5.4 miles to a microwave station road, and bear right, continuing another 2.2 miles to a dirt road at some corrals. Turn northeast and continue a quarter mile, the head south 5.2 miles to more corrals. Just before the corrals are reached, a road heads up a wash. Follow this road 3.6 miles, staying on the main track to a cabin near Railroad Spring. This remote route is for experienced desert four-wheel explorers only!

Recommended basic maps: AAA Nevada/Utah and San Bernardino County road maps; Benchmark Maps Nevada Road & Recreation Atlas. Also check individual topographic maps.

OLD IVANPAH

*"Oh, I do love these crumbling ruins. We never tread upon them but
what we set foot on some revered history."*
    ☯ John Webster

Every writer who has ever read or witnessed the sprouting of a
western mining town is so astonished that he seems to use the same
superlatives or terms of exaggeration over and over again. Truly
though, there is good reason for these superlatives in describing
Old Ivanpah. Every tattered burro man returning from that busy
camp announced:

"Richest silver I ever saw."

"If the veins hold out it will be the greatest mining town the
world will ever see!"

The frantic scramble for claims began in 1868 when three
prospectors struck a rich silver lode on the easterly slope of Clark
Mountain, just west of the Nevada border. In less than six weeks
five hundred claims had been posted and six months later more
than 5,000 were officially filed. The name of Ivanpah rolled off the
tongues of every miner from the highest peak in the Sierra to the
sandy shores of the Colorado. In just six months, Ivanpah had
grown from a stretch of barren desert to a beehive of activity.

The flanks of the hills were dotted with makeshift tents and
hastily constructed lean-tos and soon mining swung into full time
promotion. The largest mine aside from the Ivanpah itself was the
Beatrice Mine. It was located on the west end of Ivanpah Hill, three
miles north of Clark Mountain, which contains the greatest number

Ruins at Old Ivanpah. Photo: Leslie Payne

of mines in the Old Ivanpah district. This deposit was discovered in 1870 and was principally active from that year until February of 1880. During that ten-year period, the mine was owned and successfully operated by the McFarland Brothers and the Ivanpah Consolidated Mill and Mining Company. The Beatrice and the Monitor Mines   in a southeasterly direction are estimated to have produced more than $3,750,000 in silver bullion while the surrounding mines, namely the Lizzie Bullock, Allie Mae, and the Stonewall, produced roughly $500,000 worth of poor grade silver. During the ten productive years in which these mines operated, Ivanpah began to change her shabby buildings for something dressier. The rickety lean-tos were replaced by stone and adobe houses. The Whitfield Spring was diverted into many directions and small gardens grew and flourished.

Another large mine, the Colosseum, was opened and work on a heavily timbered mill was started. All the itinerant prospectors who had not done so well in other boom towns punched their burros and headed for Ivanpah. The population of Ivanpah never remained stable. Early losers moved out as the optimists moved in. The stage line made a regular stop at Ivanpah and as the whiskey, water, and conversation flowed freely, the stopover sometimes lasted for days.

Gone today are these prospectors and their faithful burros. The busy hum of the mill is stilled and the stage station is but an empty shadowed pit. The stone and adobe houses have partially given way to the slow desert growth and destructive wind force. The mills and their gigantic timbers are still undisturbed as are the lofty hills that guard a multitude of undiscovered wealth. For in the belt of crystalline rock that extends from Mesquite Pass south along the front of Clark and Ivanpah Mountains is frosty-white quartzite and rich dolomite. Occurring sporadically are fine-grained mica and garnetiferous schists. Foliated granitic gneiss is the most common rock in this region and it also takes on many colorful hues. Adobe ruins scattered about the rocky terrain and the large corral near the spring, which nourish two huge old cottonwood trees, are the most picturesque of setting for the artist.

Today you may reach Ivanpah by taking the off road that leads to State Line and following a trail that can be seen through the alluvial slope that leads up into the Clark Mountains. After eleven miles you will be able to see the two tall cottonwood trees. The road continues up Colosseum Gorge to the Colosseum open pit gold mine that operated during the 1980's and 1990's. By walking west across a shallow ravine you will come to a small canyon that was once the rip-snorting town of Ivanpah.

OLD IVANPAH & WHISKEY SPRING

CLARK MOUNTAINS

WHISKEY SPRING ● OLD IVANPAH

WHISKEY PETE'S

STATE LINE

I-15

To Baker & Los Angeles   ©2007 SDP, Inc. Map not to scale

DIRECTIONS

From Las Vegas, head south on Interstate 15 to State Line (Primm) and exit. Turn right, passing the entrance to Whiskey Pete's. Follow the old paved highway inside the fence that intersects the dry lake 4.7 miles, passing an old corral and windmill. You will have to open and close one cattle gate. Turn right on a dirt road, following it for 5.2 miles. Look for a dead cottonwood tree and many old foundations. High clearance two-wheel drive or four-wheel drive recommended.

Old Ivanpah is protected by the Antiquities Act and National Park Service regulations. Rock collecting is not permitted.

Recommended basic maps: AAA Nevada/Utah and San Bernardino County road maps; Benchmark Maps Nevada and California Road & Recreation Atlases, and individual topo maps.

JIM BEAVER'S LOST MINE

To the west of Las Vegas, deeply hidden in a lonely section of the legendary Ivanpah Mountains, is a little known lost mine. It's not a million-dollar bonanza like the "Lost Dutchman" in the heart of the Superstition Mountains or the fabled "Breyfogle Ledge." By any standards it is a golden treasure fit for any king's ransom. A clue could be a rusty pick plainly in view or a ... but then, I'm getting ahead of my story.

Along in the fall of 1860, Jim Beaver was hiking in the western slopes of the rugged Ivanpah Mountains when he ran into a dense fog that totally enveloped the usually bright hills and valleys. Nevertheless, he continued, anxious to prospect. The heavy fog held on for hours. The most skilled of mountain men can become lost in such a fog, and when this one lifted, Jim Beaver realized that he was unquestionably lost.

Now his object was to find a way out of the rugged hills and to find water. As time went by, he reached the top of a rocky pinnacle. Far to the west he spotted a clump of tall trees. The valley in which they were situated was as unfamiliar to Beaver as the lengthy hills he had just ascended. The sun had warmed the ground beneath him when at last he lay down to rest. As he sprawled out in utter weariness, his attention was taken by the shrill cry of a golden eagle perched on the bough of a gnarled juniper.

A glint of metal high on a limb of the old tree caught his eye. It was an old rust-encrusted pick resting at a peculiar angle. It pointed grotesquely at a narrow opening in a ledge above his head. Curious

Looking for Jim Beaver's Lost Mine in the Ivanpahs. Photo: Leslie Payne.

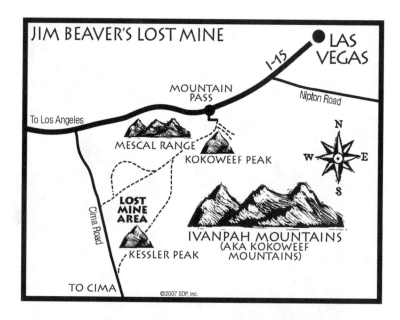

to find out more, he clawed his way to the precarious overhang. Peering into the dim cavernous opening, a golden cache filled his vision. Shining particles as big as the end of a thumb were lying in neat piles between the coarse sand and gravel on the cave floor.

Picking and digging a larger opening, Jim Beaver's eyes grew larger at the sight of several small leather pouches toward the rear of the cave. Two of the bags contained even larger specimens of the precious nuggets, while the remaining three pouches were filled with tobacco, bullets, and small scraps of unreadable paper.

Beaver's quick eyes now sought any kind of game that would ease his hunger so he could go on examining his golden find. A shot fired could attract the unwanted attention of a wandering prospector or Indian. It could mean death.

Soon he began to realize how weak hunger could make even the strongest of men, even a man who had a king's ransom within his grasp. He carefully concealed the gold in the cave again and covered the entrance with a large rock. Over this he spread dirt, silt and the dried limbs of a desert shrub. Soon the last trace of his secret was sealed.

For eight days he stumbled, searching for water and food until two miners found him barely alive. They gave him food and water, nursing him until his strength returned. In his exhausted delirium, he revealed his secret cave of golden nuggets.

He knew he could never hope to retrace his path. For years he searched in every direction. No hill or valley corresponded to the picture so clear in his mind. As the years went by, the infirmities of old age set in. Eventually, he revealed his secret to two longtime friends. As proof, he gave them two golden nuggets he had carried with him since that fateful day.

The accompanying map shows the approximate location of Jim Beaver's lost gold, if still there at all. The roads are rough and rutted. With a little luck and a reliable four-wheel drive vehicle, you might stumble upon old Jim's lost treasure.

DIRECTIONS

From Las Vegas take Interstate 15 south approximately sixty miles to Mountain Pass. Cross the bridge to the left and follow a dirt road to the Kokoweef Mine, about 6.0 miles. Go 4.6 miles beyond the mine to the Kessler Peak area in Ivanpah Mountains. For an alternate route, head west towards Los Angeles from Mountain Pass on Interstate 15 to Cima Road and exit. Follow Cima Road south to the Kessler Peak area. This area is within the Mojave National Preserve, so National Park Service regulations are in effect. Collecting of any kind, including rock collecting, is prohibited.

Recommended basic maps: AAA Nevada/Utah, California, and San Bernardino County road maps; Benchmark Maps Nevada and California Road & Recreation Atlases. Check individual topographic maps for more detailed information.

CAVE OF BLACK GOLD

A subterranean river ebbs and flows every twenty-four hours through a gigantic cavern glistening with crystal-like stalactites and stalagmites; walls that sparkle like diamonds; grottos filled with gold nuggets sifted throughout ebony sands—all hidden within the depths of a mystic cave. Does it sound like a fable? A figment of ones imagination? It is not! This cavern of gold most assuredly exists. Men have lost their lives in its bottomless depths and others have sought its untold riches, never to be seen again.

The Cave of Black Gold was discovered many years ago by two Paiute Indians and a prospector, whose identities remain unknown. These three men explored many miles of this underground fairyland, bringing with them to the surface a pocketful of golden nuggets and the body of one of the Indians who had drowned trying to ford this treacherous river. The remaining Indian tabooed the cave and never returned. The old prospector, however, journeyed to a nearby camp and told his story of the eerie cave and the sand filled with black gold. In the years that followed, another prospector named Riley Hatfield stumbled upon this same legendary cavern. Filling his pockets with gold he made his way back to a large mining camp at Crescent, Nevada, where he described the cave exactly as had the Indian and prospector before. In the late 1920's still another gold seeker was to happen upon the elusive cave. His name was Earl Dorr. It is said that he spent the last years of his life exploring the cavern. He calculated there to be more than eight miles of tunnels. At one point, the cave reached a height of 2,000 feet. The grottos were three hundred feet wide and the ledges dropped two hundred feet below the surface of the swiftly flowing waters.

The shore of the river was black sand glowing with burnished gold. For two miles this river rushed until it dropped to a deep pool far into the bowels of the earth. Fantastic? Yes, but very real, for Earl Dorr swore to all this in an affidavit in San Bernardino County in 1930. In 1959, two spelunkers lost their lives while exploring the dark tunnels of this cave.

So you see the cavern does exist and how many more there are like it we will never know, for the surrounding mountains are a veritable belt of crystalline rock that extends from Mesquite Pass to the slopes of Clark and Ivanpah Mountains. This includes Kokoweef Peak, site of the Cave of Black Gold. The fault in which the area lies contains quartzite, dolomite and granitic gneiss with fine grade mica schists. Andalusite and garnet are colorfully layered in pink quartz in the immediate vicinity of the cavern. Some thirty-five miles southeast a large cave has been opened for public inspection. Anyone visiting Mitchell Caverns State Park will readily see why it is possible that the entire region could be honeycombed with the same interesting formations. The Cave of Black Gold was taken over some years ago by a local mining company. They were said to have dynamited the only known natural entrance to the cave, yet reports handed down through the years claim there were actually two entrances. The one on the east side of the mountain that has been sealed and another to the north, near Kokoweef Peak itself. If this is true the lost entrance, it could be the one that leads to the river of gold.

On a recent trip to the Ivanpah Mountains, we discovered a small cave containing a colorful display of minerals, quartz, garnet, selenite and hornblende, and on the floor—black sand!

True the cave was small compared to the dimensions of the legendary cave but the mineral formation was the same and the black

Florine examines the rusted remains of an old car. Photo: Leslie Payne.

sand was very much in evidence. Beneath our feet we were conscious of faint rumbling sounds that could have been made by the flow of an underground river. A heavy rolling fog and light rain cut short our exploration, but we plan to return and search again for the lost entrance to the Cave of Black Gold.

DIRECTIONS

Drive south on Interstate 15, exiting at the Bailey Road/ Mountain Pass off ramp. Follow a paved frontage road east 0.7 miles to where it turns south (becoming dirt) into the Ivanpah Mountains. Continue another 1.9 miles to a fork. Head southeast (left) 1.2 miles to a road junction at the base of Kokoweef Peak. Either park here or continue to the east where mining tracks head up the east side of the peak. Stop and look in the many limestone formations. Four-wheel drive recommended. This area is within the Mojave National Preserve and all National Park Service regulations regarding camping and hiking apply. Collecting of any material including rocks is prohibited.

Recommended basic maps: AAA Nevada/Utah, California, and San Bernardino County road maps; Benchmark Maps Nevada and California Road & Recreation Atlases. Check individual topographic maps for more detailed information.

LOST BLACK ROCK MINE

In 1906, two ranchers were hunting a lost calf on a high mesa northwest of Stagecoach Spring in the Castle Mountains of San Bernardino County, California. One of the men noticed evidence of an old placer digging with many holes each about the size of a wagon box. The two continued looking for the calf. They thought no more about the discovery until spring of 1916, when two old prospectors came to the ranch, their burros loaded heavily with placer equipment.

They had come from New Mexico they said, at the insistence of their mother who was near 90 years of age. She told them their father had found a placer field many years before. He had obtained considerable gold and returned home to New Mexico. Always intending to work his find again, he drew a map that the sons inherited upon his death. This map showed a high mesa flanked by rugged hills with a winding stream bed running along its eastern edge. It lay at the rim of a large rolling plain, another stream bed along the opposite edge. No cities or towns were shown, nor were the names of creeks, rivers, or springs. Much of the information the brothers had came from their mother. She told them that the workings were about ten miles north of a place she believed to be either Hart or Barnwell, and to the west of a spring called Stagecoach.

The old prospectors, both more than seventy years of age, camped at the ranch, then began their search of the rugged territory. After days of futile looking, they came back exhausted and very disappointed.

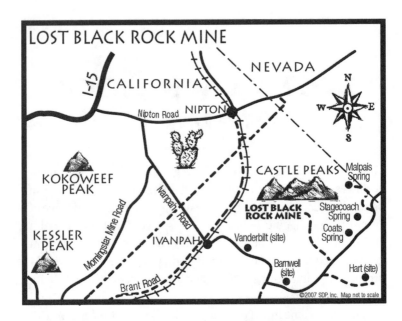

Several years went by. The rancher had come to the belated con-
clusion that the old placer bed he stumbled upon was the same one
sought by the two old men. He also concluded that coarse gold had
filtered down from an old stream in the mountains. Saddling his
horse, the rancher made a trip up the mesa to attempt to locate the
placer bed he had seen twenty years before. Memory is never as
good as a real map. The terrain had changed. Mesquite and cacti
had sprung up, water courses moved. He finally gave up his search.
Another prospector got wind of the lost placer in 1935. Although he
combed the area of Stagecoach Spring for weeks, his quest, too, was
unsuccessful.

In 1979, a friend of mine who ran cattle in Lanfair Valley told me
about this lost bonanza and said he had a fragment of the old map.
He also told me a portion of the trail marked on the map bore a
curious symbol, a symbol no one else had deemed important. My
friend, who was both an amateur prospector and cryptographer,

thought the sign to be significant. It was a crude drawing of a bird with only one wing extended. What could it mean? Perhaps someday someone will decipher the code and strike it rich.

DIRECTIONS

From Las Vegas take Interstate 15 south to the Nipton exit and turn left (east). Take the Nipton Road south 2.5-3 miles and turn south on Ivanpah Road to Ivanpah. Follow the road to Vanderbilt Mine in the Castle Mountains. Stagecoach Spring and Coats Spring are due east.

Recommended basic maps: AAA Nevada/Utah, California, and San Bernardino County road maps; Benchmark Maps Nevada and California Road & Recreation Atlases. Check individual topographic maps for more detailed information.

LOST MINE OF NEW ALBANY

Rumor has it that ghosts still guard some lost mines. There are even stories that suggest that certain ghost towns are under the care of specters that waft their unearthly beings back and forth throughout eternity. This particular story is about beings of flesh and blood that once stood guard over an old crumbling town. If rumor and fact can be combined, this is truly an unusual adventure.

In the early 1880's, when mining was the star of the west's great theater, a new town sprang into being. It was officially named New Albany, but everyone called it "Bany" for short. Men from every occupation wandered into the new settlement. Crow Daniels was one of these men. He was a miner, assayer, blacksmith, and jack-of-all-trades. To eke out a living he did a little bit of all four. Each spare hour in his busy days, he would add another stone or two to the walls of his slowly growing abode.

As time passed, Crow spent less time in Bany. Before dawn, he would be on his way to the nearby mountains. By nightfall he would return to his house. Once a month, Crow would mount his old mule and head for Crescent Camp with a small bag firmly attached to his belt. The next morning would find him on his way back to New Albany and the New York Mountains with his pockets full of coins.

Residents of New Albany knew him as "the mystery man" or as "the miser" who had made close acquaintance with only two persons in his life. The two were orphans left to fend for themselves at an early age in that rough mining camp. As generous to the two

All that remains of New Albany. Photo: Leslie Payne

boys as he was stingy to all others, Crow made for many a night's speculation and gossip in camp. This tight friendship never failed to bring a smile to even the most cynical observer.

Mining men are a peculiar lot. When the vein of ore drifts too far, they move to greener pastures. Bany's ore began to play out and her citizens followed the ore's example. Slowly the townsfolk began to move away, everyone, that is, except for old Crow and his two adopted sons.

Not long after New Albany was laid to its final rest, Crow was laid to his. True to his last request, Damon and Pythias, as he had always called the two orphans he had befriended, buried him behind his house, his labor of love. Also, true to his dying request, they stayed on in that moribund town. They left only long enough to carry a small bag to the nearest camp and to replenish their supplies.

For many years, they guarded the deserted town tucked away in its remote valley. Those strangers who came upon it quite by

accident, left in great haste. They did not wait to hear a second blast from the ancient shotgun that echoed loudly from the surrounding cliffs.

It has not been too many years since Bany claimed her last two residents. Whether or not Bany is finally at rest, just collapsed silvery wood on the desert floor, will only be known when the next passerby stumbles upon the ruins.

The laboriously constructed house of Crow Daniels may still be visible. Perhaps somewhere in the vicinity is his secret cache of gold. Maybe, too, Damon and Pythias remain true to their promise and still guard New Albany.

One of the old Mojave family ranches. Photo: Wynne Benti

DIRECTIONS

From Las Vegas, take Interstate 15 south to the Nipton exit. Go 3.5 miles and turn south on the Ivanpah Road and follow it toward Vanderbilt and the New York Mountain Road. Pass through the New York Mountain at southward into Lanfair Valley. At the OX Ranch Road, head northeast and look for old ruins. This area is within the Mojave National Preserve, and all National Park Service regulations regarding camping and hiking should be observed. Rock collecting is prohibited.

Recommended basic maps: AAA Nevada/Utah, California, and San Bernardino County road maps; Benchmark Maps Nevada and California Road & Recreation Atlaseses. Check individual topographic maps for more detailed information.

GOLD OF
SAWTOOTH WRIGHT

The jagged Sawtooth Mountains stand steeped in mystery. Desolate and stark, they seem to dare brave souls to enter them. Strange tales have been told by those lucky enough to explore them and return.

One of the strangest of such stories was related some forty years ago by a traveler at the site of old Barnwell. This traveler heard the story from a grizzled prospector to whom he had given a lift. The old burro man claimed he once knew the legendary Sawtooth Wright, an itinerant gold seeker who had roamed the desert for half a century or more. The tale is essentially as follows:

Sawtooth Wright had been hanging around Barnwell, making friends with the Paiutes who lived in the area. Rumor had it that the Indians knew of a rich treasure trove in the surrounding hills. From time to time they would go deep into the mountains and return with gold nuggets the size of a thimble.

Never daring to follow, Sawtooth nevertheless lent an attentive ear to the talk, registering the information carefully and storing it in the back of his mind. Fearing the Indians were becoming suspicious that he wanted to steal their treasure, he decided, after much deliberation, to move on. He secretly planned to return, follow the Indians and locate the cache of gold.

"I decided to travel in a circle," Sawtooth told the old prospector. "And then, when I figured no one was watchin' or follerin' me, I'd head east into the lower end of the mountains where I'd seen them go a lot of times."

"I was purty sure I'd fooled them, but one night when I was sitting by the fire, I heard something. Or did I just imagine that I heard something? I strained my old eyes hoping to see through the darkness, but I couldn't see anything. Whatever it was had disappeared."

Several nights later, old Sawtooth claimed that he heard the thing again. This time, there was no doubt in his mind that something was stalking him. However, daylight always makes the previous night's fears go away. The bright sunlight rids the desert of its goblins and ghosts, so old Sawtooth continued his search. He made his way deeper and deeper into the bleak, rocky range. Why he chose the particular spot he did to start digging, no one will ever know. After about a foot his shovel resounded with a metallic clang. In what seemed like an eternity, he unearthed an old trunk. It was filled with enough nuggets to keep old Sawtooth in luxury for a hundred years. Tears of joy streamed down his face. Being the cautious desert man he was, he carefully buried the rusted trunk again in a spot closer to a small rock cabin he built for shelter.

That night called for a celebration, didn't it? Sawtooth Wright donned his battered hat, took two of his golden nuggets and headed for the camp of the old-timers in the foothills of the New York Mountains. The celebration lasted two days and nights. On the third day Sawtooth headed back to the hills and his precious treasure trunk. Was something following him again? A small, black, shapeless thing in the distance? Tiny footprints in the sand were blown away before he could examine them. Still it trailed, and then nothing.

Sawtooth was found a week later, an emaciated corpse, partially buried by the blowing sand. There is little to add to this story, except that Sawtooth Wright firmly believed that he had seen and heard ghosts of the mountains who protected the treasure trunk of the Indians. Maybe his heart stopped cold with fear. Maybe the ghosts came to claim what was theirs. The trunk remains hidden deep in the rugged territory of the Sawtooth Mountains. Old Sawtooth's cabin would now be just a shell. And the ghosts—who knows?

DIRECTIONS

From Las Vegas take Interstate 15 south 10.8 miles past State Line to the Nipton offramp and exit, heading west. Go 3.5 miles and turn south on Ivanpah Road. At 9.5 miles is the town of Ivanpah. Turn left where the road intersects another dirt road. At 2.9 miles is the site of the old Vanderbilt Mill. 4.4 miles farther on that same road is the remains of the old railroad stop Barnwell. Sawtooth's gold is said to be in the Sawtooth Peaks (a.k.a. New York Mountains)which are visible behind the town. This area is within the Mojave National Preserve, and all National Park Service regulations regarding camping and hiking should be observed. Rock collecting is prohibited.

Recommended basic maps: AAA Nevada/Utah, California, and San Bernardino County road maps; Benchmark Maps Nevada and California Road & Recreation Atlases. Check individual topographic maps for more detailed information.

SAWTOOTH MOUNTAINS
(AKA NEW YORK MOUNTAINS)

It is a never-ending source of wonder to those new to desert country how absolutely beautiful it can be. The mountains and canyons are filled with marvelous things: gnarled and twisted trees, secret ponds of clear water, graceful birds, hidden mines, even a deserted house or two, the latter being sad little reminders of a past long forgotten.

The mountains surrounding Las Vegas are steeped in mystery. Hidden deep in the McCullough Mountains is a lost diamond treasure. Concealed within the Clark Mountains is an ancient Indian turquoise mine. The Spring Mountains hold hidden Spanish gold. The New York Mountains are said to hide great caves where outlaws once hid their loot. There are canyons that can only be reached through narrow openings and old mines that contain gold so profuse that it shines from crevices when the sun's angle is just right.

Over the years, different people have bestowed many names upon the New York Mountains. My favorite is the Paiute Indian name of "Sawtooth." Their evening silhouette is jagged and serrated just like a saw.

Recently a group of us ventured into one of the most rugged canyons in those mountains to locate the old Death Valley Mine and a tiny settlement I had discovered many years ago. Early morning found us on the Nipton Road heading for an obscure trail leading to the canyon. The geology of the mountain slopes became familiar to me as we drove along, the thrust of an outcropping, the unusual color of the rock formation; yes, this was it. As we turned onto the faint trail, we spotted two hawks nesting on a high pole, a huge

An old hopper in the Sawtooth Mountains. Photo: Leslie Payne

flock of ravens and many black-tailed jackrabbits. Climbing higher, cacti and yucca gave way to juniper and a few scattered pines. In the higher elevations, small patches of snow became visible, but the air was warm, balmy and still.

After a few miles the incredibly bad road abruptly ended. Tumbled rock guarded shallow pools where wary range cattle drank. On one flank of the hillside was a wall that many years ago had been used as a corral. It was here we had lunch before our hike up the precipitous canyon.

After lunch we explored an old dump where purple glass glittered in the sun. We found an old lantern and the remains of a crucible hand-lettered in Chinese. Fantastic rocks covered the ground — quartz, mica, dolomite granite, rhyolite, and pyrite that glowed like gold. What a colorful geological array.

All of us were anxious to see what was farther up the canyon, so off we went at various speeds. The old mine and mill were more or less intact, as they stood on a higher plateau. Time had loosened the massive timbers. Ore carts were twisted and crushed in the wash. Two of the small houses were completely gone, and the sad little graves I remembered from years past had vanished.

Yet, even with the destruction and devastation, the area is beautiful. Water that had tumbled into the clear pools had frozen and formed crystalline falls. The edges of the ponds gave life to emerald watercress. Birds dipped to drink and were not afraid. There were more remnants of the past: a purple jar, a fancy old stove, bits of painted china, a scrap of metal, a bed frame. Old foundations of stone lined the upper reaches of the canyon. Looking across the canyon we could see "glory holes" laboriously dug by some long dead prospector who once held high hopes.

The day was all too short. The sun fell behind the jagged mountains and it became cold. We hiked back down to our vehicles where hot coffee in a thermos awaited us. This was a great day spent in a fascinating area. Who could ask for more?

DIRECTIONS

From Las Vegas take Interstate 15 south about 54 miles to the Nipton turnoff. Go approximately ten miles east to the railroad tracks, but do not cross tracks. Follow the road south along the tracks. At the fifth underpass turn left and follow a trail to Sawtooth Canyon, about 4.0 miles. This area is within the Mojave National Preserve, and all National Park Service regulations regarding camping and hiking should be observed. Rock collecting is prohibited.

Recommended basic maps: AAA Nevada/Utah, California, and San Bernardino County road maps; Benchmark Maps Nevada and California Road & Recreation Atlases. Check individual topographic maps for more detailed information.

NEW YORK MOUNTAINS CAVE TREASURE

The New York Mountains are located just a few miles south of the Nevada-California border. Behind a thick growth of yucca on a steep, clifflike side of these mountains is a cave, large enough to hold a herd of cattle. According to the stories, the cave also contains a rich treasure of gold bullion and dust hidden by Indians.

According to the legend, a party of settlers was traveling through the mountains in search of a spot to settle. Though they were unable to find a satisfactory spot for a settlement immediately, they did find gold. They accumulated a great quantity of it, which they packed on their horses for transport to San Bernardino County where they would have their ore assayed.

Weaving their way through the lower reaches of the mountains on the return trip, they were attacked by a band of Indians who were more interested in capturing horses than in stealing the gold. In the surprise of the attack the horses were successfully driven away. The heavily armed settlers put up such a stubborn fight that their attackers withdrew. Driving the stolen horses before them, the marauders fled to the safety of a mountainside cave. From this stronghold they were able to hold out against the counterattack of the settlers.

The party of emigrants finally reached their long-awaited destination of San Bernardino, where they spread the news of the gold they had found, then lost, to the attackers. It was assumed that having no use for the treasure, the Indians would leave it in the cave. However, no one in the group was interested in risking life and limb, returning to reclaim it.

During the battle, many Indians were killed. Those injured, were left to heal or die. Ricocheting bullets had also killed several horses and cattle. For years, the area around the cave was marked with the bleached bones of men and animals.

A few years ago, two ranchers were rounding up some cattle in the New York Mountains when a calf wandered behind a manzanita bush. An investigation led to the discovery of a cave entrance. As the cowboys cautiously entered, they discovered the bones of animals scattered over the floor. They suspected there might be something else hidden in the cave. Being superstitious about discovering treasure that did not belong to them, they rode away without any additional search.

When other ranchers heard of the cave from the two men, they conducted a search but found nothing. What happened to the gold taken from the emigrants' horses? Your guess is as good as any.

The cave treasure story was told to me many years ago by a prospector friend of my grandfather. Known as a truthful man, he claimed to have searched for this cave, but never found it. He also told me a tale of a lost mine in the Ivanpah Mountains which follows:

A party of Paiutes was returning from their camp in the Clark Mountains to another on the northern slopes of the Ivanpahs. They had escorted a group of eastern hunters to the Clarks and were now riding leisurely homeward. They followed the Indian custom of traveling in as straight a line as possible. A few miles north of the Ivanpah Mountains the Indians came upon the skeletons of three men. The bones were bleached white by the sun, pulled apart and scattered over a wide area by predatory animals. In their midst the Indians found a shallow mining shaft, some tools, utensils and a small pile of ore generously sprinkled with gold. They picked up a few of the larger pieces to take home with them.

Skirting the western side of the Ivanpahs, they came to a waterhole at the north end of the Whiskey Spring Mountains where they stopped for the night. Later that evening an old prospector stopped to fill his canteen. He paused to chat with the friendly Indians and

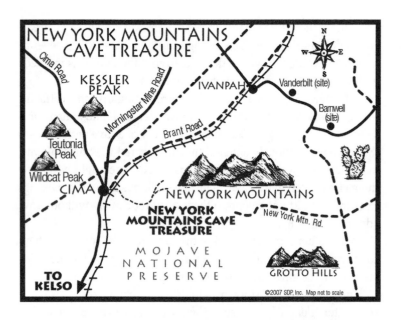

noticed the few rocks they carried. Examining one with a true prospector's curiosity, he saw at once it was rich with gold. Not wanting to arouse the Indians' interest, he carelessly tossed it aside saying it had no value.

That night he camped a short distance away. In the morning, he watched the Indians break their camp and ride away. He then returned to their campsite. As he hoped, they had left the few pieces of ore. He now examined the rocks thoroughly and verified his first opinion. Knowing the Indians had come from the direction of the Clark Mountains, he attempted to follow their tracks. At first, it wasn't difficult. Then he came to the high, rocky country north of the Ivanpahs where their tracks were lost in the boulders. He had to give up for the moment.

He took pieces of the ore to the assay office in San Bernardino. The samples assayed out at $2,000 a ton. He told no one where he had secured it. Soon he returned to the area and continued to search. The years passed. He grew old, and still he searched. Then the day came when he could no longer stand the rigorous life. It was only then that he told others, including my grandfather's friend. They also searched but never found the skeletons, the lost shaft, or anything else. I have searched the area often, but to no avail.

The far reaches of the New York and Ivanpah Mountains hold many secrets and treasures. Some are small — an intricately chipped arrowhead or a bottle purpled by long exposure to the sun's rays. Others are larger and more mysterious — lost mines, caches of gold, a mining camp or two so remote that men of this century have yet to discover it. Perhaps the next seeker to enter the beckoning canyons and hidden valleys will uncover a forgotten bonanza. It could be you or me.

DIRECTIONS

From Las Vegas, take Interstate 15 south about 63 miles to the Cima Road exit. Go south across the highway about 18 miles to Cima, California. From the railroad track any dirt roads or trails leading over the tracks or under the trestles head directly into the New York Mountains. The roads are bad to nonexistent and four-wheel drive is required. Conditions vary according to recent weather and snow blocking the roads is common during the winter months. This area is within the Mojave National Preserve, and all National Park Service regulations regarding camping and hiking should be observed. Rock collecting is prohibited.

Recommended basic maps: AAA Nevada/Utah, California, and San Bernardino County road maps; Benchmark Maps Nevada and California Road & Recreation Atlases. Check individual topographic maps for more detailed information.

196 OUT FROM LAS VEGAS

TURTLE MOUNTAINS TREASURE

Rugged, forbidding and practically waterless, the Turtle Range is an impressive and spectacular sight in the Mojave Desert. To the experienced desert rat they beckon with their many tales of lost treasures, and stories which act as fuses to detonate the inherent lust for treasure hunting. The two classic stories of the Turtle Mountains are those of two lost mines, the Lost Arch Mine and the Lost Tub Mine.

About one hundred years ago, two prospectors made their way to the Turtle Mountains with one pack animal, and two days supply of food and water. Arriving at their destination, they were faced with the necessity of finding more water immediately, or death by thirst was the grim alternative. The two men separated. One explored a narrow valley while the other entered a gorge in hope of locating a spring or even a water cache hollowed out in a pocket of rock. Both were unsuccessful in their quests, but the partner who explored the canyon returned with exciting news. Not far from the head of the gorge he found a natural bridge of stone spanning the dry watercourse. Pausing for a moment to rest in the shade cast by the arch, he idly scratched the sand with the toe of his boot. Instantly he noticed the sand was heavier than it should be. A brief examination disclosed the reason—it was half gold!

The prospectors had found wealth beyond their wildest dreams, but empty canteens dangling from their saddles reminded them that their immediate concern was that of saving their lives. With no knowledge of a water supply any nearer than the

Colorado, they turned eastward through the desert where heat waves shimmered over the gray sand. After untold hardship they arrived on the river's bank, and gulped down the tepid, muddy liquid. One of the men succumbed to the torture, the other proceeded to mining camps down the river and exhibited his gold to an astounded populace.

Only the notorious lack of water in the Turtle Mountains and its attendant peril held a major gold rush in check. Occasionally some daredevil prospector would stake his life on an attempt to find that rich placer. No records exist to show the number who tried and returned empty handed, or the number who never came back at all.

The second account tells of two adventurers who braved the fastness of the Turtle Mountains about ninety years ago, traveling in a wagon laden with barrels of water. Besides the conventional equipment for washing gold dust, they carried a tub for the purpose of catching water that slopped from their gold pans in order to conserve the precious fluid and permit them to use it in a continuous process of washing.

Their search for the golden sand proved long and arduous. In the meantime, their horses developed a thirst like that of barflies in a salt refinery and as a result, their precious store of water shrank at an alarming pace. At last, when they succeeded in digging their picks into "pay-dirt," only a few gallons of water remained. Frantically, they started to pan out what they could under this handicap and in a short time $12,000 in coarse gold was stored away in canvas bags, with an undetermined sum in fine dust left in the muck on the bottom of the tub. With barely enough water left to get them out of the desert alive, they cached the tub in a small cave near the scene of their labors and returned home.

For some reason that has never been fully explained, the men were unable to go back to that spot where they had found a small fortune. In the years that followed, scores of other individuals trekked through that rugged area searching for a narrow, sandy

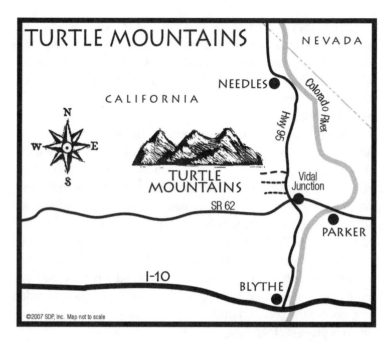

wash in a deep gorge and a small cave sheltering an old tub. So far as the outside world is aware, the rediscovery was never made, but the search gave birth to a new saga of hidden treasure, the story of the Lost Tub Mine.

DIRECTIONS

To reach the Turtle Mountains from Las Vegas, take Boulder Highway east toward Boulder City, then follow Highway 95 about 79 miles south to Interstate 40 just west of Needles. Head east toward Needles, about 11 miles, exiting at the southern continuation of Highway 95. Follow Highway 95 south. The Turtle Mountains are the spectacular volcanic mountains to the west. Various dirt roads head into the range.

Recommended basic maps: AAA Nevada/Utah, California, and San Bernardino County road maps; Benchmark Maps Nevada and California Road & Recreation Atlases. Check individual topographic maps for more detailed information.

SPIRIT MOUNTAIN AND CHRISTMAS TREE PASS

Did you ever stop to think what strangers we are becoming to the earth and its products? Have you ever wondered what it would be like if time was reversed a thousand years or more? There would be no supermarkets, no drugstores, not even a doctor. How would you feed and clothe your family or provide for their medical needs?

Thousands of years ago nomadic bands of people roamed what is now southern Nevada. They thrived on nature's resources, using every available plant, seed, and tree. Their first cultivated crop was corn, small and inedible by our standards. Squash was little better, for it was tough and stringy with a bitter taste. Those two foods must have been welcome diversions from the otherwise monotonous diet of game, seeds, and roots. In America, corn became the foundation of our flourishing civilization, but it was a long time before corn really came into its own. Until then, early cultures used wild plants in a variety of imaginative ways.

Creative cooks used the bean of the mesquite tree to make a hot cereal, grilled cakes, and dried flour. Sometimes these sweet, nourishing beans were eaten raw or fermented into a heady brew.

The resin or gum from the mesquite tree was eaten like candy, used like glue for mending clay pots, and even served as diaper material. Juniper and yucca fibers were woven into baskets, twirled into cordage and twine and woven into sandals. In the north, this material was intertwined with rabbit fur to make blankets.

Andy Zdon on the summit of Spirit Mountain next to survey marker. Photo: Wynne Benti

The hard bluish gray berries of the Juniper were dried and ground into meal and when steeped in water, they made a mildly alcoholic beverage. The seeds were also used for ornamentation on clothing and strung for necklaces. Young shoots and roots of juniper trees made an excellent soap when crushed and ground. This concoction was also used to soothe strained and bruised muscles as it reduced swelling and hastened healing.

Manzanita (mountain mahogany) was highly prized for its berries and leaves. The boiled berries made a tasty jelly and the dried leaves were used for tobacco.

Yucca was perhaps the most versatile of all native plants. Buds, flowers, stalks, and seeds furnished the Indians with their most important source of food. Baskets were woven from the stalks and repairs were made using the sharp points of the leaves as needles and strands of fiber for thread. The roots were eaten raw and pounded to a pulp and used as a highly effective cleansing agent. The root was also a mild laxative and could be used to soothe a sore throat as well. Seeds from the pinyon pine were a staple food in the Indians' diet. These were eaten raw, roasted, ground or cooked.

Although not too profuse in the southwestern desert, wild berries were occasionally found. These and occasionally wild honey, added sweets to the diet. For seasonings, early man used wild sage, horse mint, wild onions and cabbage. Salt was difficult to obtain, so a great deal of trading occurred where salt was concerned.

Meat was a welcome addition to any meal. Deer and mountain sheep were hunted with atlatl spears. Smaller game was trapped with snares. Meat could be eaten raw, roasted directly in the fire or dried and jerked for future use.

The early Indians were adept at treating minor ailments with nature's resources. Stomach disorders were treated with teas brewed from Ephedra or wild rose hips. Wounds and sores responded to a poultice of powdered cinquefoil. Yarrow was used in treatment of burns, while buckbrush and agave dulled pain much as aspirin does today.

These concoctions from wild plants and trees have been handed down from generation to generation for untold ages. An old Paiute friend of mine once told me:

"These plants are not new. They are the earth's gifts of nourishment and healing powers to man."

The Indians traveled to Spirit Mountain to give thanks for nature's bounty. The most fervid picture of an artist's fancy could not transcend the glories revealed in the heights of Spirit Mountain. Lofty spires suffused in purple haze, ebony shadows, and pale tinted walls become faintly etched in your mind. Just as you believe you have familiarized yourself with every crag and canyon, the light changes, illuminating other isolated spires and peaks. Spirit Mountain is ever in transformation, changing with the seconds from crystalline clearness to a grey slumbering haze.

The early Indians said this towering peak was inhabited by the Great Spirit. Ritual, mythology, and religion pervaded the Indians' life to such an extent that at least half their time was spent in ceremonial activities. Spirit Mountain played a leading role. Rites were performed in the nearby canyons in hopes that the Great Spirit would provide rain, abundant crops and plentiful game. Still visible on the pale walls of the canyons in Spirit Mountain are great varieties of petroglyphs — animals, natural forces, plant root systems and many religious symbols. Agricultural and meteorological symbols such as growing plants, rainbows, clouds, animals and lightning were carved into the rocks. These petroglyphs were used in ceremonies under the direction of the shaman or medicine man. The members of the tribe first purified themselves, fasted, prepared the altars, fetishes and offerings and, lastly, gathered the prayer sticks. All these symbols were thought to convey messages to the Great Spirit. The principal deities were the sun, the wind, the earth mother, clouds, and thunder. These spirits supposedly controlled the weather, crops and all phases of everyday life.

The Spirit Mountain area is most unusual. On the summit of Christmas Tree Pass, gateway to the mountain, a miniature forest erupts from the crushed granite floor. Dense and quiet, these conifers seem strangely out of place in a maze of gigantic boulders. Perched at grotesque angles, huge rocks seem to defy the laws of gravity. In many outcrops, wind and erosion have gouged deep eaves, a perfect row of sandbucket castles, and a multitude of strange figures.

Deep washes scar the otherwise smooth desert floor, giving protection to a host of spiny plants. Dropping from the summit of the pass, the Colorado River can be sighted at several points. Here in this wonderland, one feels untouched by the hurried world left behind only a short time ago. Spirit Mountain, Christmas Tree Pass, Petroglyph Canyon and the lovely blue Colorado River — all of this beauty can be found in one lovely adventure.

DIRECTIONS

Take Highway 95 south to Searchlight. From Searchlight, drive 13.8 miles south on Highway 95, then turn east (left) on the well-graded dirt Christmas Tree Pass Road. If you miss the road, Christmas Tree Pass Road is also 5.3 miles north of the junction of Highways 95 and 163 to Laughlin. Follow a good dirt road to the Pass. One can continue eastward over the pass toward Laughlin. Suitable for two-wheel drive vehicles.

Recommended basic maps: AAA Nevada/Utah, California, and Colorado River Area road maps; Benchmark Maps Nevada and California Road & Recreation Atlases. Check individual topographic maps for more detailed information.

THE GOLD OF THREE PROSPECTORS

This tale and the one following, "Lost Mine of the Clouds," were written to inspire even the most sedentary armchair prospectors to get out their picks and shovels, hire a single-jack, and start looking.

One day early in the year 1897, a party of three ragged prospectors stopped at an assay office in San Bernardino, California. Removing six large sacks of crudely stitched canvas from their pack animals, they handed them to the clerk. The bags contained more than $5,000 worth of gold.

It took the men two days to purchase supplies with their new found wealth, before heading back out of town in an easterly direction. The men had been secretive, but not careful enough. Several townspeople had been near the assay office when the three received the results of their assay and their money. Soon word of the rich ore was out. Everyone wanted to know who the three strangers were and from where they came.

Five citizens of the town decided to find out. They trailed the three prospectors to a camp in the foothills of the New York Mountains just east of the railroad siding known as Cima.

Next morning, the prospectors packed their camp and moved out, heading east. They were followed at a distance by the five observers. At a low peak, they turned and went through a pass that opened into a long flat valley. Suddenly the prospectors stopped, turned completely around and caught the five trailing men by complete surprise. Making an excuse about being lost, the men pleaded with the prospectors to take them along until they came to any kind

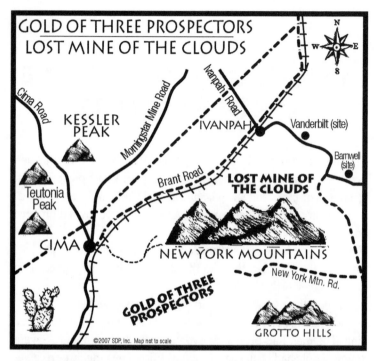

of settlement. The prospectors agreed, saying they were only a day's walk from a place they would set up a permanent camp, a place on a well-known trail.

Making a great show of establishing their camp, the prospectors worked late into the evening. Then, during the night they silently packed and rode away leaving the five followers soundly sleeping. At dawn the transgressors awoke to find themselves alone. Undaunted, they started an immediate search for tracks. Following the easy trail, they again entered the long flat valley. In the sand, they found three sets of tracks going in three separate directions. After a few hundred feet, the tracks vanished. The five had no choice but to return to San Bernardino where they reported their failure.

Shortly after 1900, an engineer doing some survey work for the state out in the East Mojave, quite by accident, stumbled across a neatly stacked pile of rich ore in a long, narrow, flat valley in the New York Mountains. The ore had apparently been sitting there unattended for some time. He gathered it up and took it down to San Bernardino to the assay office. The clerk at the office informed him that the ore was identical to ore brought in a few years before by three prospectors. They concluded that the three prospectors must have met with disaster.

As late as 1926, two men discovered another pile of neatly stacked ore in a valley in the New York Mountains. They described the valley as long narrow, and flat. That same year, two young boys out horseback riding discovered a tin can containing small pieces of gold ore. Where did they find it? In a long flat valley in the New York Mountains.

DIRECTIONS

From Las Vegas take Interstate 15 south about 54.0 miles to the Nipton exit. Turn left. In about 3.5 miles turn south on the Ivanpah Road and follow this road 9.5 miles through Ivanpah. Continue on a dirt road east to Barnwell, then from Barnwell follow an even worse road to the remains of the old railroad siding of Hart. The one way trip from Las Vegas is about 95 miles. Roads to the New York Mountains are fair to poor graded dirt. As the roads go deeper into the mountain canyons and valley, they become very poor dirt, when they even exist at all. Four-wheel drive is required, as is strenuous hiking. This area is within the Mojave National Preserve, and all National Park Service regulations regarding camping and hiking should be observed. Rock collecting is prohibited.

Recommended basic maps: AAA Nevada/Utah, California, and San Bernardino County road maps; Benchmark Maps Nevada and California Road & Recreation Atlases. Check individual topographic maps for more detailed information.

LOST MINE
OF THE CLOUDS

The old prospector who told me this story spent most of his life searching for a mine he found and then lost.

When mining activity was at its peak in the New York Mountains, towns such as Hart and Barnwell sprang up to fill the needs of miners from nearby mines and mills. It was in Hart that old Stoney Feetham lived. He had worked at a mine for a while but decided to strike out for himself. Sometime in the early part of 1900, he bought himself a burro and started prospecting, finding a few promising mineral leads.

One summer day he started out to a place he called New Albie or New Olbie, a distance of about thirty miles. It was hot as fire, he said, so from time to time he'd sit in the shade of a large yucca or mesquite. As was his habit, he would crack rocks that had fallen from ledges. One sample was rich in gold. Picking more rocks from a nearby ledge, he found more gold. He gathered what he could. After stuffing his pockets, he went back to Hart for more supplies and equipment.

When he got to Hart, he pretended that he hadn't found a thing, staying in town to chat with his cronies. Several days later he started out to work his vein in earnest, but wasn't able to relocate the ledge or fallen ore. A place he had passed so many times was now totally unfamiliar. Everything seemed to have changed. He was at a loss to explain it.

Lost mine of the clouds??? Photo: Leslie Payne

Back to Hart he went, to retrace the steps of his first trip. His money ran out and he had to go back to work. Every spare moment he had was spent looking for the lost ore. He could visualize the ledge clearly, but in reality, he was never able to rediscover its location. He spent the rest of his life searching for the elusive ledge, his proverbial pot of gold at the rainbow's end. On his deathbed, his last words were of his lost mine, "The Lost Mine of the Clouds," his friends had named it, for like a cloud it had dissolved.

DIRECTIONS

From Las Vegas take Interstate 15 south about 54.0 miles to the Nipton exit. Turn left. In about 3.5 miles turn south on the Ivanpah Road and follow this road 9.5 miles through

Ivanpah. Continue on a dirt road east to Barnwell, then from Barnwell follow an even worse road to the remains of the old railroad siding of Hart. The one way trip from Las Vegas is about 95 miles. Roads to the New York Mountains are fair to poor graded dirt. As the roads go deeper into the mountain canyons and valley, they become very poor dirt, when they even exist at all. Four-wheel drive is required, as is strenuous hiking. This area is within the Mojave National Preserve, and all National Park Service regulations regarding camping and hiking should be observed. Rock collecting is prohibited.

This is a trip for the hardy and like most excursions into the Nevada desert, should not be attempted during the summer. Gas and food are available in Nipton, Mountain Pass, State Line, and Searchlight, though gas stations and eateries are sometimes prone to short lives along this desert interstate.

Recommended basic maps: AAA Nevada/Utah, California, and San Bernardino County road maps; Benchmark Maps Nevada and California Road & Recreation Atlases. Check individual topographic maps for more detailed information.

DEATH VALLEY AREA

STUMP SPRINGS

This very name is synonymous with the choicest history that came out of the early west. History was made by determined groups of men and women who carved an odyssey into the desert. With infinite courage they suffered unbelievable hardships and deprivations that would have discouraged lesser men from the start.

Dreams of gold and untold wealth in the far west spurred them on. The Old Spanish Trail was one of the main routes to the gold fields and Stump Springs one of the main stops, where water was cool and plentiful for tired and thirsty travelers. The springs were indeed a welcome sight.

In 1844, a party headed by John C. Fremont, stopped at the springs where they found the bodies of several Mexicans waylaid and massacred by Indians. In 1848, another party from New Mexico found a similar sight as they prepared to camp by the springs. In 1851, a group of Mormon settlers headed by Captain Jefferson Hunt, camped at Stump Springs after having been driven from Resting Springs by Indians, some thirty-eight miles to the south.

It was a great deal of luck that they escaped the fate of their predecessors. At the insistence of the party leaders, search parties were sent out to scout the entire area but the search proved fruitless.

Stump Springs was also a favorite spot for countless outlaws. Caches of stolen goods and stores of ammunition were hidden in the small caves that lie partially covered beneath the mesas. Many thousands of dollars of loot was recovered as late as 1910. Today, Stump Springs is left with a legacy of violence and death, for its history was written in the blood of men.

Stump Springs tailgate picnic

Let us look through this historical spot as it is today. The springs after rains are flowing swiftly into the waiting washes, but where death once prevailed, life now abound.

Birds of all description inhabit the cool waters. The prairie falcon, marsh hawk, owl and other birds of prey frequent the springs and find food plentiful as do the small rodents and lizards that have thrived in the sandy hummock. The sand dunes and small hills around the springs are covered with the trails of the kit fox, the western cat, and the familiar coyote.

At high noon a sparkling myriad of color seems to cover the low dunes. Upon closer examination we find the ground literally carpeted with flint chips and colorful pottery left there by the nomadic Indians who once roamed through the entire region. Large fire pits are also visible as well as the worn trails that led to and from the water supply. Huge cottonwoods shade the jagged remains of an old adobe house, no doubt the labor of an early homesteader.

Here the rock hunter, the nature lover, and the spectator alike will find much to interest him. The crisscrossed back roads just seem to beg to be explored. The springs and most of the surrounding land are privately owned so there is no hunting or shooting. Pack up the cooler, a picnic lunch, bring a camera, and visit beautiful Stump Springs soon.

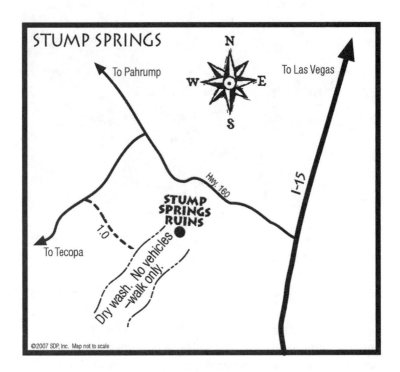

DIRECTIONS

From Las Vegas take Interstate 15 south to the Arden-Pahrump Road (Highway 160). Follow Highway 160 west about 38 miles to the Tecopa turnoff, the Old Spanish Trail Highway, and turn left. Note odometer and drive about 6.7 miles. Make a sharp left on a dirt trail and follow it for one mile to a deep wash. Park at the wash and follow the wash left on foot until another set of sand dunes is reached. Author's note: this is my favorite place on earth!

Recommended basic maps: AAA Nevada/Utah road map; Benchmark Maps Nevada Road & Recreation Atlas. Check individual topographic maps for more detailed information.

LEGEND OF LOST CANYON

Northwest of an old Indian Ranch in the Nopah Mountains of southern Nevada, along the Old Spanish Trail, is a deep canyon known as Dead Man's Wash. The place was so named because two mysterious murders occurred there. Many settlers believed the killings were the result of supernatural forces. In the early 1920's, a member of a wagon train found a man dead near the narrow mouth of the canyon. The grim discovery was enough to supply the name.

There were also stories about a hermit who was seen from time to time in the area. He ranged from Pahrump Valley in Nevada to Resting Springs in Inyo County, California. One friend related this report to me:

"I was prospecting in the mountains ten miles east of the Indian Ranch, looking for quartz with a gold fleck. A friend had discovered such a vein just months before. Looking up at the low ridges, I saw something a-setting on a rock. I got up the nerve to take a closer look. When it saw me approach, it rose. It was a big hulk of a man with long matted hair and a scraggly beard. As I got near, he turned and ran into the hills and disappeared."

Many men vanished or were said to have vanished, never to be heard from again. A young Indian woman was found choked to death at the same spot where the first murder victim was found. As the stories circulated about the two grim discoveries, prospectors and settlers ceased to enter the canyon.

Then came two gold seekers, Jack Harris and Bodie Croix. They were determined to overcome the fear and awe of the canyon to explore its innermost reaches. They had heard that there was gold, more gold than they could pack out on a burro, and they were set on finding it. Following a difficult trip through low, tangled brush, and across loose and slippery rocks, they made their way a mile into the canyon. The going was arduous. Dusk was quickly approaching. They were almost ready to turn back, when they were startled by a loud rustling sound up ahead. This was followed by the noise of some heavy object crashing through the bushes. They saw an immense animal that resembled a bear, but its legs were longer. As they watched the shape, it began to look like a huge ape more than six feet tall. They shouted and it turned toward them. It was a man, no doubt the hermit, clad in the furry skins of animals. Turning away from them, he bolted into the dense growth and was swallowed up by the darkening canyon.

Harris and Croix decided to bed down for the night with plans to continue exploring the next day. At dawn, they rose and started a complete examination of the canyon. They located several caves and dugouts. In one, was a large pile of bones, heaped with leaves and weeds. It probably served as the hermit's bed. They also found several skins and the half-eaten remains of a rabbit, but found no trace of the hermit.

As they continued up the canyon, they found a little stringer (a series of thin gold-bearing quartz veins) stuck low in the side of a hill. They decided to dig a bit at the marked location. When they were down a few feet, they came upon a flat square stone that completely covered the bottom of the hole. They enlarged the hole until they were finally able to lift the slab. Underneath was a small can with two small gold nuggets inside, a sure sign someone had located gold here.

Early the next morning, the two men set out again on their search. They were elated, thinking that they were so close to striking it rich. For five days they picked and dug on the hillside. They came up with nothing more than worthless rock. They were sure that the two small nuggets they had found the previous day, were buried there for a reason, but the question was who had so carefully buried them and why?

At last they decided to leave, somewhat disappointed because of their failure to locate the big strike. As they made their way through the torturous canyon undergrowth, they heard a low moan. Thinking it was the hermit they hurried forward. Instead, they found an old man lying on the ground, so sick he was unable to move. He, like Croix and Harris, had been prospecting and had fallen ill from sunstroke. In his feverish, high-pitched voice he managed to ask them to help find his gold specimens. Croix and Harris searched the ground five hundred feet in all directions with no luck. The old man kept muttering, insisting he'd found gold.

"Look fer it! Look fer it!" he cried. The two started looking again, crawling and sifting the rocks on the sandy floor. Suddenly Croix sat straight up, grasping a piece of rock. "For the love of heaven! He did find gold!" Harris came running and they examined the specimen carefully. It was quartz, badly shattered, but in each crack was a band of pure gold. It was enormously rich. Rich beyond imagination!

Being honorable men, they took it back to the old prospector. Barely breathing, he mumbled over and over again unintelligible words. In a few hours, he was dead. The canyon had taken yet another life.

Croix and Harris carefully wrapped the gold-bearing quartz and headed toward the old Indian Ranch, all the while planning their next trip into Dead Man's Wash.

It was almost three years before Croix was able to return. He had fallen ill and was unfit to travel. Harris lost his life in an accident. Croix finally returned to the canyon with a friend, his burros, and enough provisions to last a month. And, as all lost mine stories go, they couldn't find the lost gold. They couldn't even locate the canyon. Perhaps it had been filled by landslides, or an earthquake. Maybe a torrential flood had permanently closed the opening.

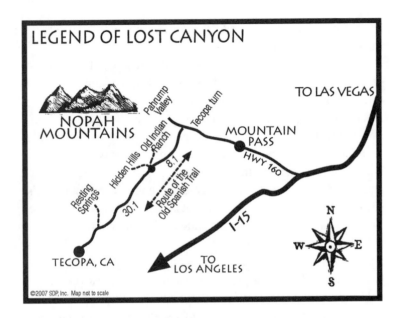

LEGEND OF LOST CANYON

There is no answer.

The story is true. The man who told it to me, told it in all sincerity. As with all desert tales, the years had put their own polish on the story. Campfires, desert nights, prospectors and tall tales all go hand in hand.

DIRECTIONS

From Las Vegas take Interstate 15 south to Arden-Pahrump Road (Highway 160). Follow Highway 160 west about 38 miles to the Tecopa turnoff which is also known as the Old Spanish Trail Highway. Follow this past the Hidden Hills area. After the road bends to the south, stay right at a fork and continue to where the road crosses the Nopah Range at Emigrant Pass. Maybe . . . just maybe, Dead Man's Wash is near here!

Recommended basic maps: AAA Nevada/Utah and California road maps; Benchmark Maps Nevada and California Road & Recreation Atlases. Check individual topographic maps for more detailed information.

STIRLING

Hidden away on a Juniper-covered hillside, is a quiet and forgotten camp of ghosts. In 1889, a gold strike broke the prehistoric silence of Stirling. The resounding clang of pick and shovel hitting the hard rock were the first modern sounds to ring out across the pinyon and juniper-covered ridges of Stirling.

Taking a shortcut from the Panamint Bonanza in Death Valley, California to the thriving Delamar camp near Pioche, Nevada, prospectors discovered a brilliant outcropping of galena housed in a most unusual blue limestone. Galena, while not as rich a find as gold or silver, still could line a hungry man's pockets and buy a good grubstake for the next venture.

Although extracting lead from the obdurate limestone proved backbreaking, most of the miners found time to do vast exploratory work in the nearby canyons. It was on one of these probes that gold was discovered in the abundant tan quartz. Bedrolls were hastily thrown together, wagons were loaded and overnight the entire population of Galena Claim No. 1 moved on up the canyon to golden pastures.

A deep vertical shaft was sunk, cutting deeply into a wide quartz vein literally webbed with gold. A huge mill was soon off the planning board and started. Heavy machinery and timbers were hauled all the way from Milford, Utah, 300 miles to the northeast. Groaning wagons were a familiar sight as they wound their way up the sloping mountainside to their destination at Stirling.

The camp boomed. Water seeped sweet and clear from the abundant springs dotting the area. The climate was cool while the

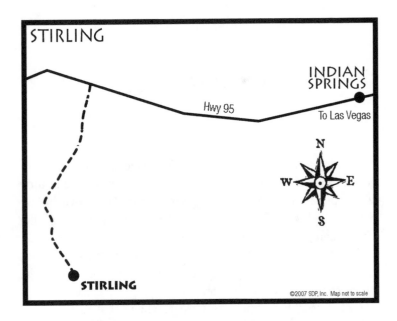

lowlands sweltered. The deeply rutted desert trail proved a magnet to the heat weary prospectors of Death Valley. Sharp investors grabbed the choice land, cleared it and resold it for a handsome profit. A tent city mushroomed up almost overnight. Streets were laid out. With a general store in the offing, miners sent for their families and Stirling was well on the way to becoming a legend. Then disaster!

World War I succeeded in shaking the world to its core. War vibrations sent shock waves reverberating to each corner of the earth. Stirling was hard hit. All mining activity ceased. The population decreased quickly. Soon the last man left and an air of desolation settled on the once promising gold camp. Sage and cactus once more became occupants of the cleared lots, while shacks and tent houses tumbled by the wayside. Speculative promoters moved most of the heavy machinery over the mountain to Johnnie, a defunct camp with little more promise of rebirth.

Nature has disguised what little is left of Stirling. Decades of wind, rain and sand have obscured the rutted winding path. A rusted pick, a fragment of bright china, and a few scattered memories are all that remains on that once busy hillside. The silence of the ages has descended upon Stirling. Perhaps some day she'll shake off the dust of inactivity and rise once more to her former glory.

DIRECTIONS

This is for four-wheel drive vehicles only. Take Highway 95 north approximately 54 miles to Indian Springs. Note your mileage at Indian Springs and continue another 11.2 miles northwest to a dirt road heading south (left) toward the mountains. Once the dirt road leaves the highway, it quickly degrades to rough dirt. Follow the dirt road about nine miles to the Stirling Mine. A cement foundation, the site of the old Stirling Mill, will be found. Some landmarks along the way include a power line that is passed 0.9 miles from Highway 95, and a wash six miles from Highway 95 that is driven in for about 200 yards and exited on the right. Four-wheel drive is helpful on these roads, although a two-wheel drive vehicle with high clearance should encounter few difficulties.

Recommended basic maps: AAA Nevada/Utah road map; Benchmark Maps Nevada Road & Recreation Atlas. Check individual topographic maps for more detailed information.

A DRINKING MAN'S TREASURE

Ever since I can remember, I've heard the phrase, "I don't know what the truth may be, I tell the tale as was told to me." I've known of this lost treasure since I was a child. I have also read about it in long forgotten books and magazines and even in some newer ones. Here is my version of the tale:

My grandfather, Bill Morley, was a railroad man who first settled

in Nevada in 1911. He was also a great wanderer, sometimes for sheer love of the mountains and the desert scenery, sometimes for a little prospecting. I suspect he wandered just to spin a few yarns of his own and to gather some tales from his old cronies.

Once he was in Beatty, Nevada, on the trail of an old car he had intentions of buying. While he was sitting at a local café swapping stories, a storm came up, as desert storms most always do, with the intensity of a full-blown tornado. One of Gramp's pals remarked that it was almost as bad as a night back in the late 1880's. A friend of his, a teamster from California, had lost his wagon, its load and four good mules. "Disappeared!" he said, "Right out from under his nose!" Gramp's friend went on to tell all the details he could recall of that strange occurrence so long ago.

Above: The Amargosa Dunes. Opposite: A wagon similar to the one lost by Lucky. Photos: Leslie Payne.

The freighter's name as he recalled was "Lucky." He was an enterprising businessman who lived by the rule "find a need and fill it," and that's just what he did to make a tidy income. He'd bring vegetables to towns that couldn't grow their own, lumber to mines situated where no trees grew, and clothing to isolated places where there were no tailors. He even brought water to spots where water was hard to find. But this particular load Lucky was taking to Beatty, Bullfrog (a real boom town), Goldfield, and Tonopah was something quite special. He had a wagonload of goods worth a king's ransom that he was going to deliver to these mining camps? Whiskey! Kegs of it. Barrels of it. Bottles of it! Yes, he had enough whiskey to make every miner in all three camps forget about their troubles and woes for many days to come.

It seems that Lucky was about twenty miles south of Beatty when the wind started to blow. As the mules hauled the rattling wagon over the rutted trail the wind grew in velocity until Lucky

couldn't see his hand in front of his face and the mules refused to go. Lucky then unhitched the animals and shooed them off, he hoped, to find shelter nearby. Lucky hid under the wagon until he decided to find another place to wait out the storm. How long he walked and sometimes crawled, he didn't know, at least an hour or more.

All that day and night the wind raged, howling up the canyons and over the mountains, whipping the plants on the desert floor to shreds. When at last dawn arrived and the storm abated, Lucky shook the sand from his clothing and hair and whistled for his mules. They didn't come. He started walking back in the direction he'd left his wagon, but it, too, had vanished. All day he searched for the mules and the whiskey-laden wagon without success. With his canteen almost dry, Lucky headed back toward Beatty.

Back at the local bar he told his story and several listeners volunteered to instigate another search. All they found was sand, sand, sand and more sand.

An unlucky walk from Rhyolite to Skidoo, a waterless canteen, and two weeks in the sun.
Photo: Death Valley National Park Museum

Whatever happened to Lucky, no one seems to remember. However they haven't forgotten that buried somewhere under the sand dunes just south of Beatty, there is a wagon loaded with some fine whiskey.

Many thirsty miners searched for this treasure over the years. My grandfather joined them on several occasions. The whiskey was worth a fortune then, but now, over a hundred years later, it must be aged to perfection. Somewhere, there is a lost treasure that appeals to everyone. This lost treasure would certainly appeal to any drinking man.

DIRECTIONS

From Las Vegas take Highway 95 north to the town of Beatty, about 113 miles. Between Lathrop Wells and Beatty, on the left-hand side of the road, the Amargosa Dunes will become visible and unmistakable. There is a road leading to them.

Recommended basic maps: AAA Nevada/Utah, California and Death Valley Area road maps; Benchmark Maps Nevada and California Road & Recreation Atlases. Check individual topographic maps for more detailed information.

CARRARA, BEATTY, AND RHYOLITE

Only a few miles from Las Vegas is an area just begging to be explored. Many people speed up the Tonopah Highway, Reno bound, and never give a second glance to Carrara, Beatty, Rhyolite, or to the other spectacular sites that abound in this region. Take some time to visit these interesting and historic places.

The Amargosa Desert is a stark area, but filled with many surprises. In the hills ten miles southeast of Beatty and 110 miles north of Las Vegas, in the heart of the Amargosa Desert lie the ruins of Carrara, once a booming marble quarry. The marble, white with black veins, was of very good quality, but so fissured it could only be cut in small slabs, making it more or less worthless. Before this was known, a group of eastern promoters worked the quarry on a large scale. They built a small town, complete with a two-story hotel and a park with a fountain in the middle. A railroad spur line was built from the Las Vegas and Tonopah Railroad to the mill, but soon they were plagued by unfortunate incidents. The power plant burned out. The railroad tracks were the wrong size and had to be dug up and replaced. Finances grew slim and expenses were heavy. Then the marble started breaking into small, almost useless slabs. The bubble burst and Carrara went the way of many other ventures.

Heading southwest and across the highway from the ruins of Carrara are the mountainous Amargosa Dunes. These dunes of remarkably uniform size are sixty percent silica, twenty percent feldspar, twenty percent calcite, and other local minerals.

The dunes have their own quiet legends and one that persists to present day concerns buried treasure. As mentioned in the previous

One of the fanciest buildings in town. Photo: Nevada Historical Society

The site of Carrara. Photo: Wynne Benti

chapter, in the early mining days, a wagon loaded with whiskey was caught in the dunes during a violent sandstorm. It was subsequently buried under tons of shifting fine sand. Many have looked for this unusual treasure, but to no avail. Perhaps someday it will come to light, or perhaps not. It makes for an interesting treasure hunt.

Heading on up the highway, we come to the picturesque town of Beatty, Nevada. Beatty was named for its founder, a man by the name of Walter Beatty who camped by the gushing water supply as early as 1904. It is said Beatty stayed in the area searching for a legendary cache of gold coins presumed to have been buried by the Jayhawker party that had crossed Death Valley in 1849. Beatty succeeded in finding much of the Jayhawker equipment, but none of their gold. Unfortunately for him, little did he realize he was practically sitting on a fabulous gold deposit, soon to be the Bullfrog Mine located in Rhyolite, just a few miles from his spring. The mine put Beatty on the map. Beatty's spring was the only source of water in the entire district.

Today, Beatty is as it was then, a pleasant lively town that has survived many ups and downs. The two railroads which once met there are gone, but the highway taking visitors to Death Valley and Reno keep the town alive.

Around Beatty, the hills are highly mineralized and very colorful. There are good campgrounds, picnic sites and just north of town are Bailey's Hot Springs where there is an R.V. park and camper area with full hook-ups and private, hot mineral baths.

From Beatty it is but a short distance to Rhyolite, a most interesting relic of Nevada's historic mining past. Rhyolite was booming in 1905, but since ore from its rich Bullfrog Mine had to be carried by wagon all the way to Goldfield for milling, and then even farther to be smelted, the town desperately needed a railroad.

Twice Rhyolite had been promised a railroad. At first, one was to be extended from a small station, Las Vegas, about ninety miles away. Grading operations were even started on a route that would curve north around the Charleston Mountains and on to Rhyolite. Then, with no explanation, grading abruptly stopped. "Why?" the folks of Rhyolite asked. The answer never came.

Then "Borax" Smith, owner of vast borax holdings in Death Valley, made a deal with the Santa Fe Railroad to proceed on a right-of-way survey north of Ludlow, California, through the tortuous Amargosa Canyon, with a spur line to the Lila C, borax deposits and another to the Bullfrog Mining District (Rhyolite). The entire town of Rhyolite was delighted.

In less than a year, the Las Vegas and Tonopah Railroad reached Beatty and finally made the steep grade to Rhyolite. Later, the Tonopah and Tidewater Railroad also reached the Beatty area.

Travelers arriving at Rhyolite were welcomed at the commodious Southern Hotel which was so modern it boasted of two baths. In 1906, the population had exploded to 7,000 permanent residents, with several hundred more in transit. Then, in 1909, the town of Rhyolite collapsed.

Today, Rhyolite's old Spanish-style railroad depot is the only complete building of large size standing. It is open to the public and houses a small display of historic items. Another tiny building houses an antique and rock shop. The famed old "Bottle House," was built in 1905 by an enterprising saloon keeper named Tom Kelly who used more than 18,000 bottles to construct the walls. It was a building material more plentiful than wood. In 1925, a movie company rebuilt the house using all the original walls. Although the house has been fenced to prevent vandalism, it is still interesting to see.

These crumbling ruins of a once proud city are a popular subject for photographers and artists. A visit to Rhyolite is an adventure of rediscovery of Nevada's past.

DIRECTIONS

From Las Vegas, take Highway 95 north. Carrara is just seven miles south of Beatty on the east side of the highway. Several old cement buildings are visible from the highway. Beatty is approximately 113 miles north of Las Vegas on Highway 95. In Beatty, turn left on State Route 374, the Daylight Pass (or Death Valley) Road. Drive a few miles west to the Rhyolite Road, passing the huge tailings piles of the recent Barrick Bullfrog Mine. Turn right on the good graded dirt road for three miles. Rhyolite's old buildings will come into sight.

Recommended basic maps: AAA Nevada/Utah, California and Death Valley Area road maps; Benchmark Maps Nevada and California Road & Recreation Atlases. Check individual topographic maps for more detailed information.

LAUGHING BEN'S MINE

If you have ever been to the Last Chance Mountains and heard strange noises as you walked through the eerie canyons, perhaps you heard the haunting voice of "Laughing Ben." Visitors to the Last Chance Range have reported hearing a low chuckle, an unexplained laugh when they knew no one else was within miles. No stranger tale has ever come out of these somber mountains than the story you are about to read.

In 1849, the usually silent hills of the desert reverberated with the cries of gold hunters, the clang of picks, the crunch of shovels and the excited "Hallelujah!" of the lucky ones. Fifteen hour days literally were as minutes in the feverish excitement of that golden year. Nights were spent around a crackling fire drinking finely brewed coffee and swapping yarns. It was here that many an embellishment was added to the tale of "Laughing Ben."

Big Ben King was the typical burro man. His face was as brown as buckskin, his hair caught back in a rawhide thong. He was as lithe and lean from years of "walk and work," as he put it. From the ever-tanned face, giant green eyes gazed steadily ahead looking always for what lay on the other side of the mountain. His Stetson, once the envy of every prospector in the gold camps, now resembled a huge, limp flapjack, decorated at the crown with a bedraggled eagle feather. No living soul had ever seen Ben without his hat. Even Molly, his cantankerous burro, seemed to have great respect for "the hat." It was the only thing she hadn't chewed to bits.

Ben was a loner, a drifter. He talked little and laughed a lot. His journeys deep into the desert and mountains were a much discussed mystery. Who grubstaked him? He was never without the necessary supplies. Where did he go on these trips? No one followed him successfully. Did he have a rich lode somewhere out there? This was the question most often on the lips of those who discussed him. Ben always laughed when asked and never got around to answering.

Many a moon passed before the gold stampede began to ebb. Prospectors, their supplies low or completely depleted, their clothes full of holes, sold their burros for next to nothing, and straggled out of the territory, that is, all except Ben. He had not only added a new pack animal to his outfit, but a solid gold pocket watch as well. Envy, greed, and even hatred greeted him at the dying camps where he had once been welcomed.

Gold can do strange things to men. Throughout the ages gold has been the curse of humankind. To gain it, men yield their honor, affection, and lasting renown. For it, they will barter their very souls. And barter their souls, they did, but let us continue.

Early in the 1850's, Ben was often seen at Green's Camp with large nuggets of gold in his possession. Greedy eyes stared at him. Whispers of treachery drifted to his ears. Until now fear of discovery had been laughed off, for Ben was cautious. Now he covered his trail doubly well. Many men had seen the fabulous gold and as time passed Ben was badgered beyond endurance. He stretched out the times between supply trips from weeks into months. One quiet Sunday afternoon, two prospectors searching the hills for ore heard a strange noise. Stopping to investigate, they spotted Ben hurrying toward a distant mountain ridge. Advancing slowly and stealthily, the two men followed Ben until dusk settled over the remote valley. Tired and hungry, nevertheless, they struggled on in their evil pursuit.

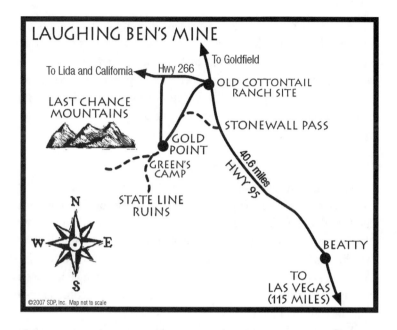

When time seemed to have lost all meaning, Ben stopped and began to unload Molly. It was here, with all caution thrown to the winds, when the two pursuers jumped into view. Ben King, startled, but quick on the draw, shot one man through the heart and turned toward the other, but too late. Ben was knocked to the ground by a large rock thrown directly at his temple. Blood ran in rivulets on the sandy ground and on Ben's beloved hat. Molly, terrified by the odor of death and violence, bolted straight for the open desert, flapping ore sacks spurring her onward.

Several days passed before the lone survivor of that fateful night reached a camp and related his grisly tale. The ground was hard where he had dug the two lonely graves, a task that had taken a full day. He searched for Molly but couldn't find her. Lastly, he combed the surrounding territory for any trace of Ben's mine. He found nothing.

A score of fortune seekers have since attempted to locate Ben's elusive mine. Either it is so well concealed that it is impossible to see, or perhaps Ben was not at his final destination. The night he was waylaid, he may have only been making camp for the night. No one ever found poor Molly. Except for the low, mocking laugh that has oft-times been reported in the area by travelers, quiet now reigns in the region.

DIRECTIONS

From Las Vegas take Highway 95 about 52 miles north past Beatty (about 165 miles from Las Vegas) to State Route 266, and turn left (west). Drive about 7.2 miles to the Gold Point Road and follow the Gold Point Road 7.6 miles to the old town of Gold Point. Follow the dirt roads past Gold Point and reach Green's Camp in 2.5 miles. At a fork stay right to the Stateline ruins. The road can be followed to the Last Chance Mountains. Roads in this area are confusing so consult your detailed maps.

Recommended basic maps: AAA Nevada/Utah, California and Death Valley Area road maps; Benchmark Maps Nevada and California Road & Recreation Atlases. Check individual topographic maps for more detailed information.

JEAN LEMOIGNE'S MINE

Death Valley abounds in mystery. Tales of lost mines and lost men are handed down from one storyteller to another. Each adds his own embellishments to the tale until it at last reaches such colossal proportions that it finally bursts and slowly trickles away. The passing years obliterate all thoughts of that once important story. This is the case of Jean Lemoigne's lost mine.

Ballarat is now a crumbling ghost town, but in its heyday it was the wildest, hell-raisingest, rip snortingest town in the valley. It claimed most of the gals, gold and gunfighters. Life was exciting. "Never a dull moment in Ballarat," Shorty Harris, Death Valley's beloved sage, often stated: "Why, even the ghosts are afraid to show their white sheets around here," he went on to say. "I once knew a man who worked the graveyard shift at the Coffin Mine in Dead Man's Canyon in the Funeral Mountains of Death Valley. If that isn't enough to scare anyone, the guy's name was Pete Bones."

Another resident of booming Ballarat was Jean Lemoigne, who was perhaps almost as famous for his coffee as he was for his silver. Lemoigne's recipe for the brew was "plenty of coffee and damn little water." From one end of the valley to the other, coffee is still judged by Jean Lemoigne's standards.

Lemoigne settled in Ballarat in early 1880 and began the inevitable search that eventually led him to the galena deposit the Shoshone Indians had worked for many months. He filed a claim on it in February of 1882 and for years was able to extract so much rich silver from his claim that his dream of returning to France was soon to become a reality. He decided to sell the mine to the highest bidder. An offer of $200,000 was made and Lemoigne accepted. "But," he stated emphatically to the buyer, "I sell only for cash." The terms were agreed upon and a check for the entire sum was offered, but Lemoigne pushed it aside. "This is not the cash. You go to town, get me the cash. I got work to do." The disgusted buyer left, never to return. Lemoigne went back to his mine and his dreams of "Gay Paree."

Summers seem endless in the desert. The glaring sun turns water to vapor and the greenery to dust. On one of those sweltering days a young Shoshone Indian came into Ballarat and excitedly cried to Shorty Harris, "Lemoigne gone! He left for his mine. Did not come back!" Shorty left to find his friend, and in the bottom of the infernal valley found a set of tracks he identified as Lemoigne's. Following the trail to Cottonwood Spring he came across a pistol he knew belonged to Jean Lemoigne. Two or three miles along the trail, he ran into Death Valley Scotty who was staring in horror at the half-eaten body that was once the Frenchman. The scavengers of the desert had been frightened away before their ghastly meal was finished. Nearby were the remains of his faithful burros who had chosen to stay rather than run off.

Lemoigne died in the valley where he had found work, success and contentment, ending his dreams of returning to his native France. Scotty and Shorty buried him where he lay, and on this day began the century-long story of the secret of Jean Lemoigne's Jinxed Mine. Six men were to die mysteriously in their separate attempts to locate Lemoigne's claim.

The first to start the ill-fated tale was Wild Bill Corcoran, who had made and lost a fortune in Rhyolite. Anxious to reestablish himself in the good graces of his creditors, he discounted the intense heat and with only his burro for companionship, set out for the Owens Valley. Reaching Darwin, he felt quite ill, but believing a nip of the old red-eye would cure anything, he secured a bottle and went on. As the temperature soared, so did Bill's fever. Four days later he was found, the red-eye gone and with it, his life.

The north fork of Lemoigne Canyon. Photo: Wynne Benti

Tex Johnson was number two. Indians came upon his bleached bones and buried them under the sand. One after another, four others followed Corcoran and Johnson. Each died before reaching Lemoigne's claim. The Indians tabooed the mine and a hush of superstition veiled the area. Prospectors cut a wide swath around the ridge owned by the black bearded Frenchman and they spoke in whispers about Jean Lemoigne and his jinxed mine.

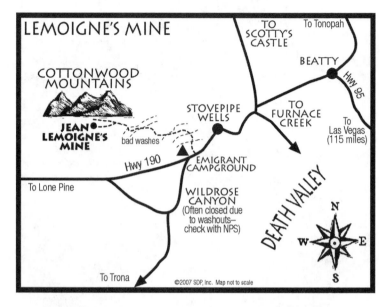

The small cabin near the mine slowly crumbled and fell, the ravages of time taking their toll. Passing years eventually diminished peoples' fear of the region, yet they were still reluctant to explore the mine. Early in 1910, a brave soul known only as "Slim" ventured into the flanks of the hills where the claim had been. He was never seen or heard from again. The jinxed mine had taken yet another life.

When darkness envelopes the valley, ghostly lights can be seen glowing on the mountainsides. Are they (as many believe) just a phosphorescent rock easily explained by science? Is it only the wind that causes the low moan to echo again and again during the night? I prefer to think the wandering spirits of Jean Lemoigne and his followers still linger in the forbidding valley and that the flickering lights are there to guide them on their eternal quest for silver.

DIRECTIONS

If you are of brave and adventurous spirit and would like to try your luck, here is your chance. Your starting point will be Stovepipe Wells on Highway 190 in Death Valley, the closest settlement to Lemoigne's claim. Stovepipe Wells has all the amenities including a ranger station, gas, restaurant, motel, camping facilities, swimming pool, and a small store. Check your mileage and drive approximately six miles west on Highway 190 from Stovepipe Wells toward Emigrant Springs, or for precisely, drive to Wildrose Station on Highway 190, then backtrack 3.1 miles east to the Lemoigne Canyon jeep road on the north (left) side of the road. Follow the extremely rough route about five miles to the marked road end. Four-wheel drive may not be enough for this route - make sure your vehicle has high approach and exit clearance as the road drops in and out of several washes suddenly, and hanging up on your bumper or undercarriage could be a very real problem. We have used a Toyota four-wheel drive pickup on several occasions without incident. About 1.5 miles from the highway, look for a very obscure trail on the right. This was the trail used by Lemoigne and his loyal burros to carry silver to Emigrant Springs.

The canyon can be enjoyed in complete solitude, much like it was in Lemoigne's day. From the parking area, walk a short distance, and you will see that Lemoigne Canyon has two forks. The right fork takes you deep into the Cottonwood Mountains and to the backside of massive Panamint Butte. Take the left fork (south fork) about 3.5 miles up the canyon (carry at least two quarts of water). The best time to hike in Death Valley is from late fall to spring. Do not attempt this walk during summer. At the foot of the Cottonwood Mountains, a mine tailing dump can be seen. A climb on foot to the mine entrance will take you back in time. Is the jinx still at work? I really couldn't say. Just heed my warning. Watch out for the ghostly lights on the mountainside. You wouldn't want to be jinx victim number eight, now would you?

Recommended basic maps: AAA Nevada/Utah, California and Death Valley Area road maps; Benchmark Maps Nevada and California Road & Recreation Atlases. Check individual topographic maps for more detailed information.

PANAMINT GOLD

We Americans are interested in our past. It lies so tauntingly close, just a short breath beyond yesterday. In the gold rush era, over a century ago, it was inevitable that rich lodes would be found and then lost and never rediscovered again. The fables of lost mines go back as far as the days of the Spanish explorers. There is unquestionable proof that some of them do exist. Some have been found and renamed. Others are called new strikes. All of them have a common trait; they are the richest of bonanzas, solid gold or silver, shining bright as the sun and just waiting to be found. All you have to do is simply stumble upon them.

"Just beyond that mountain," a seasoned prospector will inform you. "Yes, just beyond that mountain."

I wish "Seldom Seen Slim" were here to refresh my memory about the lost gold of the Panamints. My memory needs no jogging to remember the three days I spent with Slim searching for it. As for the legend, I will do the best I can without my old friend to guide me.

It was late in the summer of 1925 when Slim and his partner were on the eastern flanks of the Panamints en route to Ballarat. After deliberating for some time, they decided to try a short cut directly over the mountains by way of an unfamiliar canyon.

Two months passed before they stumbled into Ballarat. Both men were in agony from thirst, hunger and fear. The sun had blistered and baked their skin and had sickened them almost to death. Less experienced desert travelers would never have survived. Their account of the trip was rambling and incoherent. Snatches of sentences, fearsome words, "lost, no food, water, can't go on…" pierced the hearts of the small group of prospectors who met the two emaciated wayfarers.

Time worked its magic, and in less than a month Slim and his partner were back on their feet. They were able to recall most of the events that transpired in their two months of wandering across the Panamint Mountains.

The impulse to wrest gold or silver from the earth is one of the driving forces in man's make-up.

"This must be why me and old Pard decided to hunt up a few nuggets on our trek across the Panamints," Slim told me.

"Coming from the desert up to the high country was like being transported to another world of forests, deep shadowed canyons and clear water dashing over the tumbled masses of rock. The temperature was in a constant state of change, soaring to over 100 degrees in the canyons and dropping to near freezing at night. And the storms! The wind would rise and moan and begin shifting sand and dirt. Above the swirling mass the sun would become all but obliterated. The peaks of the mountains, usually so well-defined in the distance, were just a blur. As bad as the storms got, sometimes the blazing sun was a lot worse.

"We always thought our destination would be over the very next hill or ridge. Well, this one day we were on the eastern fringe of a dry, sandy canyon when the wind came up again. We tried to bear against it. We veered, zigzagged, stumbled, fell and crawled. We lost all sense of time and direction. We knew we were hopelessly lost and would need a lot of luck to get back alive.

"The wind grew stronger and we finally huddled down against the earth. After what seemed like a very long time the wind lulled. Sharp fragments of rock bit deep into our skin as we lay on the ground. We could finally see, but as far as our eyes could scan, the horizon was unfamiliar. The sky which had so recently been filled with choking dust and stinging sand was now clear."

The author examines old mine ruins high in the Panamint Range. Photo: Leslie Payne

"The ground beneath us, well, it was covered with gold nuggets. The little rocks were solid chunks of gold! We picked up as many as we could carry and started out again in what we guessed to be the right direction."

Burning days and freezing nights passed and they recognized not a single landmark. And thus they went on for sixty or more days of deprivation, judging their course by the position of the sun and stars.

The nuggets? Who knows when or where they dropped them or threw them aside. They had forgotten the fearful price a man often pays for the desert's gold. The windblown sands covered their tracks and the subsequent rains obliterated them completely.

Maybe it was the grueling trip, maybe it was just age, but before Slim and his old Pard could try to retrace their steps, old Pard passed away. Did Slim return to search for his treasure trove? Yes, many, many, times, but the search was always fruitless. He never again saw the golden rocks that lay in the sandy wash.

Shortly after the trip Slim and I made into the Panamints, he died, joining the ghosts of blanket and jackass prospectors just beyond the next ridge.

DIRECTIONS

From Las Vegas take Highway 95 north to Lathrop Wells. Turn west on Highway 373 and go 23 miles to Death Valley Junction. Take Highway 190 west through Death Valley past Stovepipe Wells. Turn south on Highway 178 and drive 30 miles to the ghost town of Ballarat. Two-wheel drive vehicles are okay. The town is now privately owned. The last time we visited, there was a small store in operation. There are many interesting four-wheel drive trips into the Panamint Mountains that start at Ballarat.

This is a rather long drive from Las Vegas for a day trip, so the seeker of Ballarat should anticipate either camping overnight, or finding lodging in Death Valley, Panamint Springs or nearby Trona and Ridgecrest.

Recommended basic maps: AAA Nevada/Utah, California and Death Valley Area road maps; Benchmark Maps Nevada and California Road & Recreation Atlases. Check individual topographic maps for more detailed information.

LAST CHANCE LEDGE

Pegleg. Breyfogle. Lost Cabin. Lost Mormon. Blue Bucket. These names can set tongues wagging in a congregation of idle miners. They are the legendary leaders among the lost mines of the West. As tradition would have it, almost every dying prospector was permitted a glance at these huge bonanzas, then from that day hence, their locations were concealed forever.

Each golden cache has its following of true believers. Each is reputed to have taken a toll in human lives as men persisted in the search for its fabled treasure. These tales may be as true as the most enthusiastic searcher alleges. Some may be figments of many imaginations. Some may have been rediscovered time and time again. However, with the rich float skimmed off, the finder never realized that his discovery was indeed the lost bonanza of his dreams. Many of these lost mines have been persistently hunted for generations. Barely a year passes without some treasure-seeker establishing himself at a camp from which he searches day after day for that illusive pot of gold at the end of the trail.

Just within the boundaries of Panamint Valley stands a sentinel, not of burnished gold or titanic carved stone, but of silvery weathered wood. This small cabin's yawning windows mock the rust encrusted lock on the sagging door. Behind it rises the pockmarked hill from which Last Chance Peters extracted a fortune.

Another lost mine? Not by any standards. It is a mine that almost anyone can locate if inspired, but they must overlook a mysterious death and a solemn warning.

Rock walls of an old miner's abode found near Last Chance. Photo: Leslie Payne

Back in 1929, Last Chance Peters and his partner, whose name remains unknown, were traveling in Panamint Valley on their way to Beatty. After some deliberation, they decided to take a short cut near the old Skidoo Road. Five months later they entered Beatty with a large bag of ore samples they had picked out of the unyielding earth.

"Gold worth at least $15,000 a ton," the assayer told them. So back they headed, hurriedly retracing their steps to the tiny shack they had erected during their stay as protection from the elements. The shack stood exactly as it had been left, but a huge landslide had buried their rich ledge under tons of rocky debris.

Despite the heat, Last Chance and his partner dug. They literally clawed the hard earth until fever and frustration claimed the life of Last Chance's partner. Nearly insane with failure, Last Chance decided to return to Beatty again to replenish his dwindling supplies. What happened to him from that day on remains a mystery.

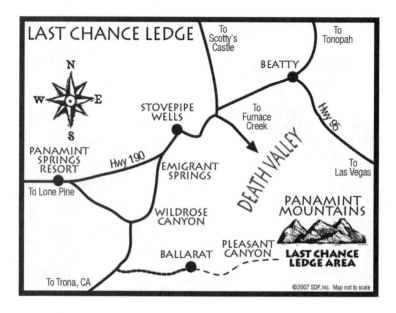

Some Timbisha Shoshone claimed they saw a ghostly apparition in the Panamint Range on moonlight nights; grim warning, perhaps, to other treasure seekers who would take his gold. Many have tried and many have failed to find the "Last Chance Ledge." Who knows — perhaps you'll be lucky.

DIRECTIONS

Last Chance Ledge is said to be in the area of Pleasant Canyon, above the Ghost Town of Ballarat in the Panamint Mountains. Pleasant Canyon is south of Surprise Canyon and north of Goler Wash on the west side of the range. Four-wheel drive is required in Pleasant Canyon. The road is rock-stepped and washed over by an ephemeral stream at the mouth of the canyon. Beyond that point, the road is steep, poor dirt subject to washouts, but can be bypassed with care.

Porter Peak is located at the top of Pleasant Canyon on the crest of the range and makes a wonderful dayhike or an overnight trip.

Gas and food are available at Trona, Panamint Springs Resort in Panamint Springs and in Death Valley National Park at Stovepipe Wells and Furnace Creek. There are a few active mining claims in the Panamint Range, the largest being the Briggs Mine north of Goler Wash, however, most of these will be phased out since the passage of the California Desert Protection Act in 1994.

Recommended basic maps: AAA Nevada/Utah, California and Death Valley Area road maps; Benchmark Maps Nevada and California Road & Recreation Atlases. Check individual topographic maps for more detailed information.

LOST SILVER OF OWENS LAKE

It was in 1864, when steamships were introduced to California lakes. The "Governor Blaisdell" was launched on Lake Tahoe to carry lumber for the busy mines. When mine owners realized how much could be saved in freight costs and time, steamer transport spread rapidly to such lakes as Mono, Owens, Donner, Walker, Pyramid, and Klamath.

In 1872, Owens Lake was the third waterway in California to use steamers. That year the whole Owens Valley was a hub of activity, with the rich Cerro Gordo Mine in the Inyo Mountains pouring silver-lead ore into the Swansea smelting plant. In the course of a day the plant produced one hundred and fifty eighty-three pound bars of bullion from each of its two furnaces. This added up to 25,000 pounds every 24 hours.

Props for the mine tunnels and charcoal for the furnaces came from mills and kilns across the lake in the Cottonwood Creek area. It took teams of twelve mules five days to move a six-ton load of bullion from the Swansea plant across the sandy desert to a shipping point at Olancha. This process was time consuming for anyone who shipped goods including the miners, ranchers, produce growers, and lumber mills. It was inevitable that a better means of transport became available.

On the Fourth of July in 1872, the steamer "Bessie Brady" was launched on Owens Lake. She was eighty-five feet long, had a sixteen-foot beam and a six-foot hold. The craft was powered by a twenty-horsepower 10'x10' steam engine. With a speed of just more than seven knots, it was able to make the run from Swansea to

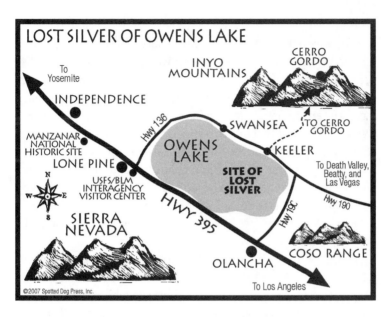

LOST SILVER OF OWENS LAKE

Cartago in three hours or less, carrying crew, passengers and seventy tons of ore. This freight cost less than half of what one wagon team charged for a six-ton load.

Under this revolutionary mode of transportation, production at Cerro Gordo Mine rose to a fever pitch. In 1877, a second steamer was introduced to Owens Lake. It was smaller than the Bessie Brady and was christened the "Mollie Stevens." Soon both ships were busy making runs across the lake, but the end of the boom was already in sight. By 1878, the Mollie Stevens was permanently moored. One year later the Bessie Brady was hauled ashore and stripped of her machinery.

There are many stories to be told of the ships' journeys between the years of 1872 and 1879. When the Bessie Brady was retired, stories of storms, silver bullion, and lost treasure endured. Here is but one of the tales told about Bessie and her sister ship, Mollie Stevens.

Bleak clouds shrouded the Sierra Nevada. Winds approaching gale force roared across the slate gray surface of Owens Lake, whipping the water to foam. A small ship was caught in heavy swells generated by the sudden violent storm. Daylight was fading as the small vessel fought valiantly against Nature's forces. Suddenly there was an ominous rumbling in the hold of the ship as the massive pile of silver bullion bars was wrenched loose and thrown across the sloping floor. The ship lost balance. Spinning and bobbing, it went over on its side, sliding the crew and the heavy silver into the depths of the lake. When the storm passed, the wind died down, and the waves ceased their churning, the lake once more regained its placid surface, covering the cargo of silver with a cloak of silt and many feet of water.

By the 1930's, Owens Lake had dried up. Many treasure seekers who had heard the story went out to find the fortune, but none were successful. As years passed and more sophisticated treasure hunting devices were invented, new searches began with metal detectors, electronic probes and other implements.

Today, the silver is still buried deep beneath the lake bed. Or was it ever there to begin with? Like all lost treasure stories, much embellishment has been grafted on to the legend through the years. If the story is true, then add a few other facts that have been passed along. Some claim to have sighted a huge propeller when the sandy bottom of the lake is swept by wind. Glints of large pieces of metal (silver?) have been seen near what were once the reefs and shallows.

True believer that I am in treasure stories, I went to Owens Lake several times armed with probes, metal detectors, shovels, binoculars and other tools that might aid in such a search. It was a delightful trip. Profitable? No, but a delightful trip.

The drive to Owens Lake is through marvelous country and even if you don't find the elusive sunken silver, I guarantee you'll have a wonderful time looking.

Cerro Gordo, high in the Inyo Mountains. Photo by Andy Zdon

DIRECTIONS

From Las Vegas, take Highway 95 north about 87 miles to Lathrop Wells. Turn south on Highway 373/127 to Death Valley Junction, 23 miles. Turn northwest on Highway 190/136 and drive about 116 miles through Death Valley, passing through Furnace Creek, Stovepipe Wells, and Panamint Springs (last services before Lone Pine). Not a mile past Panamint Springs is a dirt road to Darwin Falls, a very pleasant side trip which includes a nice short hike to the falls. To visit Darwin Falls, turn left at the sign and follow the dirt road about 2.4 miles to a parking area on the right. From the parking area, follow the footpath down into the wash and turn left (south). Follow the wash through thick willows and growth to the beautiful granite falls. Continuing on Highway 190 from Darwin Falls, you might want to make a side trip into the interesting old mining town of Darwin, home to several of Inyo County's hardy residents.

About 13 miles past the Darwin town junction, massive Owens Dry Lake will appear on the left (southwest). Across the lake, the magnificent Sierra Nevada stretches from Olancha Peak as far north as one can see. At the junction of Highways 190 and 136, you have a choice of two different routes around the lake. Turn left on

The old train depot at Keeler marks the end of the line for the Carson & Colorado, which started at Mound House, Nevada. Photo by Wynne Benti

Highway 190 to Olancha along the southern edge of the lake, then turn right on 395 to Lone Pine.

Your second option is to continue straight on Highway 136 along the eastern edge of Owens Lake another 17.6 miles to Lone Pine. Highway 136 passes the well-graded but very steep road to Cerro Gordo on the right (note the magnificent ruins of one of the many old mills in just off the road). At least a day can be spent exploring the old ghost town of Cerro Gordo on the crest of the Inyo Mountains. As of the first printing of this book, a bed & breakfast was operating at Cerro Gordo. The historic town of Keeler is just across the highway on the shores of the lake. Buried in the drifting sand dunes of the Owens playa, the ruins of old Swansea, another mill town is a few miles north of Keeler. Old mines and abandoned stone ruins can be seen in the rocky foothills above these towns.

Recommended basic maps: AAA Nevada/Utah, California and Death Valley Area road maps; Benchmark Maps Nevada and California Road & Recreation Atlases. Check individual topographic maps for more detailed information.

INCISED STONES
EASTERN CALIFORNIA MUSEUM,
INDEPENDENCE, CALIFORNIA

Among all of the strange symbols inscribed on rock by ancient cultures, it would be difficult to find any more mysterious or fascinating than incised stones. Thousands of years old, these small stones have just recently been brought to light. A dozen or more sites located in southern Nevada disclosed quite a few of these unusual aboriginal works. Although these small, flat and irregularly shaped decorated pieces were primarily etched into sandstone, limestone and steatite were also used.

These striking ancient works present distinctive features found nowhere else. Many museums specializing in Native American history have never seen incised stones, despite their great antiquity. In fact, some museums aren't even aware of their existence.

Many educated persons in the field of archaeology believe they may antedate history and tradition. Principally of one common design, these incised presentments differ only by the presence of many figures or by their absence. Some stones are quite stark, while others are inscribed with a bewildering maze of lines and circles.

Three to six inches square is the average size of the stones. They vary greatly in shape, and seem to have no distinctive characteristic form. A stone is usually divided into two sections by one or more tiny zigzag lines. Above this intricate division, is a series of "hummocks" or mounds, representing mountain ranges, perhaps. Tall stem-like lines intersected by many tiny lines present a treelike appearance. Half-circles or clefts near the base of the mounds resemble the mouth of a cave or a niche carved into a hill. Did the designers essay a sundial, a calendar, a token of thanks to the Great

Incised stone

Spirit, an amulet for good luck, or a random notion without any significance? Perhaps they are maps to specific landmarks—springs or hunting areas. Will we ever know what prompted these painstaking works? They are so marvelously done that the toil entailed in their execution is almost inconceivable.

Some experts believe them to be tokens of thanks for a good crop of pinyon nuts. Incised stones are often found beneath these cone-bearing trees. However, it is common to find them lying in the wide sandy wastes of a wash or on the chiseled crest of a dune.

Upon examination of more than 400 stones in southern Nevada, no one seems to know precisely what the figures represent. They are not idle doodling and they are much more than a good luck piece. All agree that they are one of the most intriguing mysteries around.

Dr. Carl Schuster, a noted archaeologist who studied incised stones, theorized that some of the designs were ceremonial representations of clothing. Lines seemed to indicate stitched seams and fringes. He believed that the human identity of the design was established by the depiction of personal ornaments such as necklaces. Others do not agree. Unfortunately, Dr. Schuster died before his work was completed. His papers were sent to his native Sweden.

I began observing incised stones many years ago when my Paiute friend, Russell "Buster" Wilson, showed me a site he located in the Spring Mountains. Together we explored the area by foot as time permitted. Not withstanding our progress, the task of deciphering the riddle of these mysterious stones had only just begun, so scant was the previous research.

Henry Raub, retired curator of the Eastern California Museum in Independence, California and Dr. Clement Meghan, formulated logical theories. They concluded that the people who incised these stones brought the technique of incising and the method of giving this unusual type of offering with them when they crossed to the Americas from Asia. The designs used here are similar to some found in Alaska, China, and Japan.

Leslie Payne and I have observed many incised stones zones at various elevations, from sea level to 5,000 feet, near cooking areas called "mescal pits." Many of the stones found in these areas display a pine tree design. Judging from the pot sherds, flake debris, and tools found in proximity, I would say these stones were incised anywhere from 200 to 2,000 years ago in this part of southern Nevada. The only fact agreed upon by most experts is that the incising was probably done with crude, needle-pointed stone tools called "burins" chipped from quartz or obsidian.

These relics of prehistoric southern Nevada have a story to tell of the long vanished people who made them. Hopefully, someday we will understand just what that story is.

DIRECTIONS

From Las Vegas, drive north on Hwy 95 to Beatty, Nevada. Turn west on Nevada Highway 374, which becomes 190 in the California. Follow 190 west through Death Valley, passing Stovepipe Wells, Panamint Springs and Darwin. Stay right on Highway 136 at the southern end of Owens Lake and follow it to Highway 395. At this intersection, is the InterAgency Visitor Center on the southeast corner, with excellent information and books about the local area (and restrooms). Turn north on Highway 395, passing through the town of Lone Pine. To the west is Mt. Whitney, highest point in the contiguous U.S. Continue about 18 miles along Hwy 395 to Independence, passing by Manzanar National Historic Site. In Independence, turn west on Center Street across from the Inyo County court house, where Charles Manson and his gang spent some time during the 1970s following their capture. Take Center Street to its end in the parking lot of the Eastern California Museum, location of the largest collection of incised stones in the country.

Incised stones are protected under the Antiquities Act, and collecting them is strictly prohibited by federal law.

Recommended basic maps: AAA Nevada/Utah and California road maps; Benchmark Maps Nevada and California Road & Recreation Atlases. Check individual topo maps for more info.

HOT SPRINGS AND MIRAGES

HOT SPRINGS AND WATERING HOLES

After a day of hiking and exploring, there is nothing that feels better than a good long soak in a hot spring. From earliest times man has sought the soothing mineral waters of natural hot springs to ease his aches and pains. Modern humans are no exception.

Tecopa Hot Springs are acclaimed as some of the finest. In the late 1880's, the little town of Tecopa in Inyo County, California, grew primarily because of the lead and silver mines in the nearby hills. When the Tonopah & Tidewater Railroad made its appearance, the town attracted a diversified populace, for it then proved easier access to the healing waters of the springs, one and a half miles south of town.

Native Americans and prospectors following the trails from Death Valley used the water for years, stopping mainly in winter months. The water temperature ranges from 108 to 109 degrees and has a flow of about two hundred and twenty-five gallons per minute. It tastes of soda and common salt but it is not disagreeable and may be helpful for many ailments. Today the waters are confined in covered bathhouses and are free to the public. Campgrounds are plentiful and weather is generally good during the winter months. Many devotees of the springs stay several months at a time. As swimsuits are not allowed in the public baths, several motels offer private rooms with hot baths.

North of Tecopa Hot Springs in the southernmost tip of Death Valley, and at the foot of the Black Mountains, lies a fascinating spring called Saratoga Springs. In the early years it was a swimming hole and popular meeting place for prospectors and desert travelers. Today, however, swimming is not allowed in the springs. The pool is inhabited by a small, rare fish called *Cyprinodon macularius*, or Pupfish, and they are the reason for the no swimming rule set by the Federal Government and National Park Service.

The principal spring forms a pool twenty-five feet by thirty-five feet and is three feet deep with a sandy bottom. Water can be seen rising in a dozen or more places. The temperature of the water is eighty-two degrees. At three other points along the base of the hills one hundred to two hundred and fifty yards northward from the main pool, water has been obtained by excavating into the slopes. An area of marsh grass and tules extends six hundred yards from the spring, but on account of the great amount of evaporation the area of open water varies with the seasons.

The water tastes distinctly of alkali but has formed no noticeable alkaline deposit. The mountains to the northeast consist of hard altered limestones and sandstones that dip twenty-five to fifty degrees east. Some granitic rock is also exposed at the base of the slope. Like many other ranges of this region, the Black Mountains appear to be a faulted block where the intrusive dioritic rock has produced conditions that permit the escape of water from a moderate depth. It does not seem possible that Saratoga Springs is supplied by water from the Amargosa River or by deep alluvial water that surfaces, for the water temperature and its freshness compared to water from the river do not favor either source. Even though there is no swimming allowed, it is a beautiful spot.

Devil's Hole is located just outside Ash Meadows, Nevada. Ash Meadows is part of the Amargosa Valley between the Spring (Charleston) Mountains and the Amargosa River at the base of the Funeral Mountains. It is bounded on the south by Eagle Mountain and on the north by the Nopah Mountains. Of all the springs along the edge of this dismal waste, Devil's Hole is the most interesting. It is a large, deep pool at the bottom of a natural rock tunnel, a treeless spot concealed in a wall of solid rock.

Devil's Hole is thought to connect with Big Spring by an underground passage. The two springs are only a few miles apart. Big Spring is a round hole in the floor of Ash Meadows containing living water and reported to be bottomless, as is Devil's Hole. Many strange stories have been told throughout the years. One is about a Paiute Indian woman who was washing her clothing in the "hole." A witness claimed to see her lean far over the edge to retrieve an article of clothing and just disappear. He ran to the pool just in time to see her feet disappear into the tunnel. Four days later her body was pulled from another underground spring in Tecopa, over forty miles away.

Another time, a bale of well-tied hay was said to be thrown into the Devil's Hole and it, too, reportedly appeared in Tecopa a week later. Who knows? Maybe these early stories were true, maybe not.

This next tale is true, for I was there during the search. In the early 1960's, a good friend of mine reported that her son and son-in-law had gone scuba diving in Devil's Hole several times. They had explored the large pool and decided on their next trip they would attempt to follow the unexplored and uncharted tunnel. They donned their gear which included tanks, masks and fins. They carried underwater lights. These young men were experienced divers, yet they never surfaced. In fact, they were never found.

For ten days, the Clark County Search and Rescue Team looked for them. Navy scuba divers were called in from San Diego. Other professional divers volunteered their time, but all was to no avail. The boys were swallowed up in the eerie depths of Devil's Hole, never to be seen again. Shortly afterward the menacing waters were securely fenced off and locked up.

Devil's Hole has also been the center of controversy between the government and farmers. Water that was pumped from underground sources for agricultural purposes greatly lowered the level of the pool, threatening the lives of the rare Pupfish. The matter was taken to court. The farmers lost and the Pupfish won.

Warm Springs, nine miles from Glendale, Nevada, is only forty-eight miles north of Las Vegas. Huge palm trees and cottonwoods make the area a paradise for dry desert dwellers. There is a large pool surrounded by shady trees and dotted with secluded picnic areas complete with tables and barbecues. The water gushes in and out filling the pools with fresh water every six hours. It is tepid all year around. Small streams crisscross the manicured lawns and wilder areas where birds, frogs and other small animals abound. Small natural pools and waterfalls offer wonderful spots for relaxing. There is also an area for overnight camping. Warm Springs is privately owned and there is a fee for use.

If you are heading toward Utah instead of California, you may want to stop at Pah Tempe Hot Springs, another great place to unwind. Not only does Pah Tempe have a huge pool filled to the brim with highly mineralized, soothing sulphur water, there are three small pools dug into the mountainside called "The Grotto." If this isn't enough to lure you to this lovely oasis, there is the gushing Virgin River, a wonderful picnic area, camping, cabins to rent and mountains to climb.

At 50,000 gallons per minute, Pah Tempe has the greatest flow of mineral water in the world, coming from twelve thermal springs in the Hurricane Cliffs. The primary minerals of the Pah Tempe springs are calcium, sulphur, magnesium, natural epsom salts and sulphate. The combination of these minerals works as a cleanser for the skin, removing all old soap from the pores. Where most mineral springs are troubled with some toxic metals such as arsenic, Pah Tempe has none. Many guests at the springs swear the healing waters have helped a variety of ailments such as arthritis and rheumatism.

Further into Utah is another marvelous hot spring, "Veyo." Glen Cove was its first name, but when the post office discovered there were two Glen Coves in Utah, the second had to change its name. The Mormon women in the community decided to change the name to Veyo. Some say it is the first initial of each of the women. Others say the name is an acronym: "V" for vigor, "E" for energy, "Y" for youth and "O" for oneness.

The Veyo Pool and Resort is surrounded by grapevines, towering poplars, and an enormous silver maple tree the original builder brought from Kentucky. The shaded oasis was opened in 1927 and with the exception of one three year hiatus, it has been run by the Cottam family ever since. The 30'x72' pool's temperature varies from a warm ninety-three degrees to a cooler eighty-three degrees.

These are but a few of the watering places of the desert that are wonderful to visit. After a ride across the brown and gray desert, they appear like bright green jewels scattered here and there. I guarantee they'll draw you just as they have drawn travelers from earliest times.

DIRECTIONS (FROM LAS VEGAS)

TECOPA HOT SPRINGS

Take the Blue Diamond-Arden-Pahrump exit (Highway 160) on Interstate 15. Drive approximately 48.0 miles to the Tecopa turnoff in Pahrump Valley. Turn left and continue another 27.0 miles to Tecopa and the signed hot springs. Paved road all the way. We recommend getting a copy of the AAA San Bernardino County and Death Valley maps.

KEOUGH HOT SPRINGS

Take Highway 95 north to Highway 266 and turn left. At this intersection is the old Cottontail Ranch building, one of Nevada's most famous brothels, now out of business. Follow 266 up into the Silver Peak Range, over into California to the junction of Highway 168 at the south end of Fish Lake Valley. Follow 168 over Westgard Pass and down into Big Pine. Turn north (right) on to Highway 395. Go about 9 miles and turn left on Keough Road. The developed springs are at the end of the road on the left. The free "clothing optional" hot ditch and various pools is on the right (north). Hotel, RV, and camping accomodations about 6 miles north in Bishop.

SARATOGA SPRINGS
From Interstate 15, exit at Blue Diamond-Arden-Pahrump (Highway 160). Drive 48 miles north on Hwy. 160 toward Pahrump Valley and turn left at the signed Tecopa turn-off. Continue another 27 miles to Tecopa, then Shoshone. Take Highway 127 south for 16.9 miles. Turn right (west) on a graded dirt road (about 3.9 miles south of the Dumont Dunes OHV Area). This is the southern unpaved and unmaintained route to Death Valley National Park. Follow the road north 5.9 miles to a fork and turn right. Drive 2.7 miles, then turn left at another dirt road which is followed approximately 1.3 miles to the spring. Four-wheel drives make this an easy excursion.

The southern unpaved route into Death Valley is a very scenic drive that can be followed to Highway 178, just north of Jubilee Pass. Before reaching Highway 178, the road crosses the Amargosa River several times and overlaps a segment of the historic Harry Wade "escape route," so named for the patriarch of one of the families traveling with the infamous Bennett-Arcan party who, in 1849, had to be rescued from Death Valley on their way to the goldfields of California. Harry Wade left the party and took his family south by wagon in hopes of picking up the Old Spanish Trail. Their route turned west at Wingate Wash, now inaccessible to sightseers since becoming part of China Lake Naval Weapons Center. We recommend using the Benchmark Maps Nevada and California Road & Recreation Atlases.

DEVIL'S HOLE
Take Highway 95 north about 41.0 miles to Lathrop Wells. Continue 25.2 miles farther to a sign that reads "Ash Meadows." Turn left and drive 11.0 miles to Devil's Hole on a well-graded dirt road.

WARM SPRINGS
Take Interstate 15 north to Glendale, Nevada. Turn left at the Warm Springs-Moapa sign. Drive 9.0 miles to springs. Paved road.

PAH TEMPE

Take Interstate 15 north past St. George to the Hurricane exit. Follow the main road through Hurricane toward La Verkin. Watch for the Pah Tempe signs on the right (east) side of the road. The roads are paved until the Pah Tempe turn. It's a short jaunt to the springs over good gravel.

VEYO

Take Interstate 15 north to St.. George. Exit and follow Highway 18 north to Veyo, about 25.0 miles from St. George. Good paved road all the way.

ANCIENT SHORELINES

One of the finest specimens of fossil agate I have ever seen came from the desert. It was found on an ancient shoreline formed centuries ago when the face of the earth looked much different than it does today.

Old shorelines are found in many places. They surround the dry lakes of Southern Nevada and for the collector of fossils, gemstones, and other precious items they offer a rich field of search. There is a great variety of agate, jasper, and other stones, more than can be found on any ocean shore. Without even having to get one's feet wet, the observer may find shells, coral and plant forms imprinted on stone millions of years old.

Fossils found among these pebbles represent several geologic ages. Some date back to a time when there were no vertebrates. What was once an ocean bed dried and was forced upward by the earth's movement, becoming the top of a mountain. Rivers and streams carried bits of rock from these mountains back to the shoreline of still another ocean where they were worn smooth and cast up on another shore. In our southwestern desert, following many such cycles, these water-worn rocks found their way to the bed of a tremendous river or gulf which drained much the same way the Colorado River does today.

High on the tablelands and hillsides above the course of the Colorado are the ancient beaches of this great prehistoric waterway. They extend along a plainly marked basin from the Mexican border to Nevada and perhaps farther north. Some of the pebbles found can be traced to fossil beds as far north as Montana. It is believed that others were brought from northern Canada by glaciers.

The observer will not be impressed by the first sight of these gems because they are concealed beneath a coating of "desert varnish." While these pebbles appear to be all alike, close study will reveal a great variety of color and pattern under the surface. Brilliant red and yellow jaspers vie in beauty with carnelians and banded agates. The diligent collector may even find water-worn crystals of amethyst, topaz and quartz. Even gold-bearing ore has been found, but the veteran collector knows gold will never be found in paying quantities in such deposits.

One stone generally overlooked on these beaches is black onyx. This gem was popular in former years as a setting for diamonds. Black onyx is merely a trade name for a nearly jet black chalcedony. Much of that used in the period of its popularity was artificially colored. Pieces of agate or chalcedony with a somewhat porous surface were selected by gem traders and steeped for months in hot sugar water. This was followed by soaking the stone in sulfuric acid. The acid decomposed the sugar imprisoned in the pores of the stone and left a black residue of carbon. The blackest of these stones were sold under the name "Black Onyx." The desert beaches can yield enough to supply the entire world with black onyx should it ever again become popular.

The carnelians in these deposits are usually small, but some of them are very fine in color. Occasionally moss agates are found, but the stone of outstanding interest is fossil agate.

Until the novice collector becomes familiar with fossil agate pebbles, it is likely he or she will pass them by as their beauty is concealed beneath an uninviting exterior. Most of them have a white, lime-like coating under the brown varnish surface. They appear to be opaque until they are cut. Then comes a surprise, for the stone that appeared to be merely a dirty piece of limestone often turns out to be translucent with a light pink or tan body and white or black markings.

These marks may be the outline of a sea shell, a bit of coral or the flower-like design of a cross-section of a crinoid stem. Some contain fossil prints of prehistoric plants. A microscope will bring out hidden beauties of design in all of them.

Readers should not get the impression that they may walk out on the desert and pick up nicely colored gemstones at random. The desert does not flaunt her jewels. They are there, but only for the painstaking student and collector who is knowledgeable and willing to devote time and work to the search.

An exceptionally fine deposit is on the Arizona mesa bordering Chemehuevi Valley between Parker and Needles. By odd coincidence, the eastern shore of Lake Havasu follows very closely the coastline of an ancient sea, so for those who like to go boating it is possible to ride directly to the places where gem pebbles may be picked up.

For those who are not expert collectors but are interested in the natural phenomena of the desert, the places mentioned offer worthwhile objectives for a pleasant excursion. Desert beaches have no cooling surf to offer as an inducement, but neither are they crowded with people and litter.

DIRECTIONS

Two excellent and easily accessible dry lakes are located just off the Boulder Highway on the Searchlight Road. The other is Jean Dry Lake, south of Las Vegas on Interstate 15, just east of the interstate near Jean. We recommend using the Benchmark Maps Nevada Road & Recreation Atlas.

Mirages

Once, while driving with my photographer friend, Leslie Payne, we noticed a housing development being built atop the mesa overlooking Riverside, Nevada. An entire block of condominiums was under construction, its plywood walls in various stages of completion. Some units had exposed two-by-fours, while others were nearly done, lacking only siding or paint to finish them off. As we commented on how surprised we were to see such a project, it disappeared before our eyes. We had seen a mirage!

When we hear the word "mirage" most likely, we think of a shimmering pool of water stretched across highway pavement or a desert dry lake. The concept of a "mirage" was first introduced to Europeans by Napoleon's soldiers during their campaigns in Egypt. The same kind of mirage that Napoleon's men witnessed in the sands of the Sahara Desert can be seen closer to home. On a hot summer day, if your eye is at the right level, you will perceive shimmering "water" overlying a stretch of asphalt or concrete pavement.

Bending rays of light, divided by sharply contrasting density and temperature between adjacent layers of air create a mirage. The desert mirage is the result of the formation of a shallow layer of warm, rarefied air over ground heated by sunshine. This layer acts like a mirror and the apparent water is a reflection of the sky. The effect is even more realistic when trees or other objects are included in the reflection.

Very different effects are produced by the formation of a layer of abnormally dense air over a cold surface such as water or ice. In this case, if the observer is within the dense layer, he may see an inverted

Mirage or reflection on Panamint Dry Lake? Photo: Andy Zdon

image in the sky of some distant, low-lying object such as a ship. He may see two images, one inverted and the other upright. Taller objects, such as hills and mountains, extending above the dense air will seem to be lifted above their true positions, a phenomenon known as "looming."

There are other possible combinations of warm and cold layers. A lateral mirage is formed by the occurrence of an abnormally warm vertical layer adjacent to a wall or cliff. This effect gives a distorted appearance to objects seen through it.

Lastly, a mixture of masses of air of different densities may give rise to the complex phenomenon of "Fata Morgana," the phantom city. The traditional home of the Fata Morgana is the Sicilian shore of the Straits of Messina. Many descriptions have been published of the urban apparition with its innumerable towers and palaces which bears the name of legendary King Arthur's sister, the enchantress Morgan Le Fay. The appearance is a very distorted image of objects across the straits seen through alternating masses of heated air. Similar spectral cities are observed in other parts of the world. When I was very young, my grandfather and I saw such a city against the Panamint Mountains in Death Valley. It was a wondrous experience. Some of the most striking examples of Fata Morgana have also been found in the Arctic and Antarctic.

Mirages are familiar sights to sailors, and probably explain the legend of the Flying Dutchman and other strange tales of the sea. There are accurate descriptions of this phenomenon that read like fairy tales. An Arctic voyager wrote a vivid account of seeing his father's ship inverted in the sky. With his glass he could make out details of masts and hull, though the vessel was thirty-four miles distant and nearly fifteen miles beyond the horizon. Recorded during Colonial times, was an account of a ship due to arrive at New York's harbor from England. One Sunday afternoon, following a violent storm, she was seen floating in the air. Every detail of the ship was represented so clearly against the sky that there was no question as to the identity of the vessel. She was painted in the clouds, but she never showed up at the harbor. The apparition was all that was seen of the ill-fated ship, lost at sea.

In the history of polar exploration, there are two cases in which mirages gave rise to faulty geography. In the first case, explorers were led astray by a mirage. They subsequently charted the coast of the Antarctic continent in the wrong place, thus starting a controversy that raged on among geographers for generations. The second case was that of the mythical "Crocker Land" which Peary thought he had discovered in 1906. "Crocker Land" was drawn in on the Arctic maps for many years until it was proved to be nonexistent. Several expeditions that went to the Arctic observed the same "Crocker Land" mirage that had mislead Peary.

I observed a second unusual mirage in Death Valley. Across the vast salt flats was a train of four wagons each pulled by a team of mules. The drivers wore red shirts and the feet of the animals stirred up great puffs of dust as they continued their endless journey. I could see the canvas wagon tops flap and ripple. Just as suddenly

as they had appeared, they vanished. Seeing a mirage was as thrilling an experience then, as it is now.

DIRECTIONS

If you drive past a dry lake bed on a hot summer day, be sure to look for phantom water and trees. Two good dry lake beds where mirages are commonly seen are Jean Dry Lake and Sarcobatus Flat Dry Lake. To get to Jean Dry Lake, take Interstate 15 south about 30.0 miles from Las Vegas. Just past the town of Jean on the east side of the highway is Jean Dry Lake. This lake is known for water, trees and freight train mirages. Sarcobatus Flat Dry Lake is located along Nevada Highway 95 between Beatty and the exit for Highway 72 on the west side of the highway. We recommend using the Benchmark Maps Nevada and California Road & Recreation Atlases.

Another classic Southern Nevada road. Photo: Wynne Benti

DESERT TRAVEL

TRAVEL SAFE

DESERT ROADS

Traveling along desert back roads can be dangerous. Always let someone know your plans. Be sure to contact local land management agencies before your trip to check on conditions. If you become stuck or your car breaks down, don't attempt to walk away from your vehicle, particularly if its hot and the walk is many miles. The people who know about your trip will know where to look for you assuming no one else happens by to lend a hand. It is much easier for a search party to find a car than a solitary hiker. Once, while on a college field trip in Death Valley, our van happened to get a flat tire along a hot, dry, and seemingly unpopulated expanse of dirt road. We were dismayed to find that a lug wrench and jackstand were not included with our van, and we had no way of changing the tire. Instead of taking on the hot afternoon sun and hiking out, the group decided to stay put. We had our camping gear, and plenty of food and water. To our surprise, within a few hours, a van load of tourists happened by and allowed us the use of their equipment. The timing of their arrival was perfect for them too. They discovered they also had a tire going flat!

Sudden flash floods can cut across roads. A dry wash can become a raging torrent, rivaling a large mountain river, in a very brief period of time. If venturing more than a few miles beyond frequently traveled roads, a party should consist of not less than two cars, with much more gas and water than you expect to use. When venturing onto the desert back roads, check the condition of your vehicle first. Start with a full gas tank, check the fluid levels, tire pressure and wear, and the condition of your hoses. The Bureau of Land Management recommends that the following equipment be carried in your car: a basic tool kit with a full socket set, pliers, wrenches, screwdrivers and the like; spark plug socket; wire cutters; vice grips; channel locks; allen wrenches; hammer, knife, spare tire and jack; a tow strap; first aid kit; duct tape (one of the world's great inventions); shop manual for your car; air pressure gauge and tire inflater; shovel; fire extinguisher; flashlight and batteries; jumper cables; and three gallons of water per person plus five gallons of water per vehicle.

The ultimate goal of everyone who makes a trip to the desert should be to come and go without leaving a trace of their visit. Stay on established roads and obey all land management agency signs concerning road access. It really is important to stay on established roads and not to cut new ones through the desert scrub. The desert doesn't get much rain, so it can take decades for destroyed desert plants to get enough water to grow again. A sport utility vehicle (SUV) or all terrain vehicle (ATV) that leaves an established road just once, does devastating damage that can last for a century! During spring, native and migratory birds build their nests in desert shrubs. The author has seen nests crushed by SUV wheels that left an established road because the driver didn't know how to drive through a stretch of sand or was too lazy to get out of the vehicle and do a little road work to make the established route passable. If everyone who owned an SUV, did what the television commercials suggest (drive gonzo off established roads), the desert would be a gutted, irreparable mess. The Bureau of Land Management has set aside desert areas specifically designated for Off-Highway Vehicle use.

ARCHAEOLOGICAL SITE ETIQUETTE

Nevada's historic sites are very fragile and easily disturbed. They must be treated with care, respect, and left intact so everyone can enjoy them. The following guidelines have been established for visitation to archaeological sites:

1. Viewing a site from a distance will reduce the impact a site receives. Stop, look and think before entering a cultural site. Locate

the midden area (the trash pile) to avoid walking on it. Middens are very fragile and contain important archaeological artifacts and information about the ancient residents.

2. If a trail has been built across a site, stay on it to reduce the effects of destructive erosion. Don't camp near or on ruins.

3. Leave artifacts in place. Make a note of their location and report them to rangers or visitor center personnel.

4. Enjoy rock art by sketching or photographing it, but don't touch, chalk in the outline, take rubbings or latex molds, or otherwise touch rock art. The slightest touch will leave damaging acids and oils from the skin on the rock.

5. Walk carefully when visiting ancient or historic structures to avoid damaging archaeological and structural features of a site. Climbing on roofs or walls could, in a moment, destroy what has lasted hundreds of years.

6. Leave all objects, including seemingly insignificant broken bits in place. The relationship of artifacts to each other and to their natural surroundings is important to any archaeological investigation

7. Writing, spray-painting, drawing on, or scratching into the surfaces of prehistoric rock art found on walls, caves or in other environments is punishable by federal law.

8. Collecting artifacts on the surface or by digging is against the law.

9. Notify BLM rangers or other authorities if you witness any illegal activity. The Archaeological Resource Act of 1979 provides stiff penalties and a reward for information that leads to a conviction.

10. Archaeological sites are places of ancestral importance to Native Americans and must be treated with respect.

MINIMUM IMPACT VISITATION & CAMPING

The goal of all who visit Nevada's beautiful desert country should be to come and go without leaving any trace of their presence upon the fragile terrain of the desert wilderness. Keep your traveling group small. Camp in established campsites away from fertile soil and vegetation. If someone has already built a firepit, use it, and resist building a new one. Here are a few pointers for camping in the desert:

1. Plan your trip well. Know where you are, where you are going and let someone know when you plan to return.

2. Good campsites are found not made. Camp at least 200′ away from any water source. Carry extra water in your vehicle. If using natural springs for water, fill your water bottles during the day and avoid using desert water sources at night since most desert animals are nocturnal and congregate at water sources after dark.

3. Stay on established trails. Don't cut switchbacks, which erode and damage trails.

4. Carry out your trash. There is no backcountry trash service in the beautiful, remote deserts of the southwest.

5. Build tub fires, or use existing firepits.

6. Keep pets leashed.

7. Bury human waste at least 200′ from any water source in a hole four to six inches deep with the same diameter. Wash dishes, yourself and anything else at least 200′ away from any water source.

8. Don't burn toilet paper! Bury it or pack it out in a zip-lock plastic bag. Entire forests have been burned to the ground by out of control toilet paper fires.

TEMPERATURE

Deserts can have an enormous temperature range within a twenty-four hour period. Under certain conditions, a few hours may be the difference between a freezing dawn and a 100-degree day in a shadeless canyon exposed to the direct rays of the sun. Long-sleeved, wind proof garments should be carried to protect from the cold, wind, or direct rays of the sun. Take short but frequent snack breaks every forty-five minutes to an hour of hiking, and wear a light-colored broadbrimmed hat. During late spring, summer, and early fall (in the lower elevations) hike when the trails and canyons are shaded, usually from dawn to late morning or from late afternoon to dusk. Avoid hiking in the sun, and in particular, avoid hiking uphill during the hottest part of the day. When we climbed Avawatz Peak in the Mojave Desert (during early summer), we started hiking around four in the morning, making for some very pleasant hiking. By the time we reached the car shortly before noon, the temperature had risen to over 100 degrees. If there is water to spare, dousing the top of one's head every forty-five minutes can be very refreshing on a hot day.

Always check ahead with the National Park Service, United States Forest Service, Bureau of Land Management or other managing agencies for pertinent route and weather information. Conditions are constantly changing. Roads may wash out due to flash flooding. Drifting sand or unexpected snow can also make them impassable. Road crews may not have signs up which notify of closures on maintained roads, and don't expect to see signs warning of closures on unmaintained roads. There is no substitute for common sense when traveling and exploring the backroads and mining country of Nevada.

WATER
Water is the most important item on any desert trip. We recommend carrying at least two 2.5 gallon containers of water for trips of two days in duration for two people. Always carry two separate water containers. We were once climbing in the desert mountains of Utah, miles away from any water source, when by accident, we stuck an ice axe through one of our containers. As we searched for the duct tape we should have had in our tool kit, all the water drained out of the container. Luckily, we had a second container.

EXPLORING OLD MINES
The deserts and mountains of Nevada have been prospected for their minerals since before the Civil War. Shafts, tunnels, rotted timbers, and rusted debris are reminders of those early days of mining. With bits of shiny purple and blue glass catching the sunlight, it is hard to resist exploring the old camps, with their intriguing histories.

When you walk the same footpaths and drive many of the old routes traveled by some of the west's most historic and colorful characters, you'll take a step back in time to Nevada's frontier past. Take only photographs to remind you of your visit. Resist the temptation to "become part of history" by carving, scrawling, or otherwise defacing these old structures as a "remembrance." Carry out all of your trash as there is no garbage service in Nevada's beautiful desert country. Bury or carry out toilet paper. Don't burn tp as range fires are expensive and time consuming to put out, and you may get caught in it!

With the help of the Nevada Division of Minerals, Bureau of Abandoned Mine Lands, we have put together a few pointers that will help you to safely enjoy the many fascinating historic mines described in this book.

EXPLOSIVES

We once camped at Panamint City, an abandoned mining camp near the crest of the Panamint Mountains (described in the chapter "Panamint Gold") in Death Valley, to climb Sentinel Peak and to explore the ruins of the old townsite. One of the guys on our trip found a cache of dynamite left behind during the last modern prospect of Panamint City in the early 1980's. The area was subjected to an intense flash flood and the residents had to get out in a hurry. Blasting caps had been tossed in some old barrels standing outside the "man" camp. We discovered them when one of our party attempted to burn some trash in one of the cans. The caps began to explode like firecrackers. When we got back down to the valley, we called the Inyo County Sheriff who is trained in handling these situations. Over time, explosives destabilize. Only trained experts should handle them. If you find explosives, don't touch them. Leave the area as soon as possible and report your discovery and its location to local law enforcement.

SHAFTS, CAVE-INS, AND ROTTEN TIMBERS

Nature erodes and weakens what is exposed to rain, sun, and wind. Weakened timbers or eroded soils around mines are usually not readily visible. Rain dropped by summer thunderstorms will move down any sloped surface, wearing away its strength. The edge, or collar, of a mine shaft can be extremely unstable, worn away by years of water and wind erosion. These collars have been known to collapse unexpectedly, dragging down anything or anyone who happens to be standing too near. Most shafts are quite deep and a fall is usually lethal. If a person survived such a fall, getting back out would be a challenge. Mine tunnels are also susceptible to cave-ins, which can be caused by minor disturbances such as talking or walking.

The old wood support timbers which were used to stabilize the mine workings a hundred years ago, today are probably rotten, weakened from decay and termites. A well-timbered mine opening may appear solid , but in reality, it may just barely be supporting its own weight. Touching a timber might even cause a tunnel to collapse. Wood ladders and stairways, the flooring, walls and ceilings of old structures are suspect as well. Years of exposure weakens wood and rusts nails.

Often times, the floors of tunnels can be obscured by murky pools of water on their surface. Imagine stepping in a pool and falling into a shaft hidden beneath its surface — quite unpleasant. The water in mine shafts and tunnels may also be contaminated with various chemicals and heavy metals.

Remember the phrase, "canary in a coal mine?" When mining was in its infancy, before technology improved safety below ground, miners used canaries to detect poisonous gases. Canaries were extremely sensitive to "bad air" which could kill a miner with no warning. When the canary passed out, the miners knew they better hightail it out of the mine. Even today, deadly gases accumulate in low areas or along the floor of abandoned mines and will initially go unnoticed. These gases can be stirred up with even the most seemingly insignificant activity — walking or talking. They can even be disturbed by a slight breeze. The bad air combines with good, and creates a potentially deadly mixture that can cause rapid dizziness, unconsciousness, even death. In addition, many mines closed due to fire. As a result, abandoned workings may be oxygen-deficient.

FLASH FLOODS & WASH-OUTS
The storms of winter bring snow to the surrounding mountain ranges and high passes of Nevada. Often, the high passes can be closed for a few hour, days or weeks due to heavy snowfall. The desert easily absorbs the winter snow which comes to rest upon its bone-dry surface, with plenty of time to melt.

By comparison, summer thunderstorms bring enormous amounts of rain to the desert within just a few hours. The desert terrain with its sun-dried soil, cliffs of limestone and basalt can't absorb the massive amounts of water deposited by these thundershowers. It is these summer storms that have the greatest potential for creating unpredictable, destructive and potentially deadly flash floods. In a matter of hours, they can turn a sudden, dry creek into a torrential river full of desert debris.

Chances are, if you are not inside a car, you will hear a flash flood before seeing it. A thunderstorm has its own sounds — first an oppressive quiet, followed by the sound of rain and thunder — a crack of lightning across the creosote plain. The sound of a flash flood has been compared to that of a jet or plane passing high and fast, but instead of getting fainter, the sound grows louder as the flood approaches.

Move to high ground, above washes and low areas. Flash flood water moves fast and carries with it debris — silt, rocks, trees limbs, uprooted cacti, and whatever else may be in its path As it passes by, you can see the rocks it carries bobbing up and down below the surface of the water and you can listen to them clatter as they strike against each other.

RATTLESNAKES, SCORPIONS AND OTHER CREATURES

Many venomous creatures live in Nevada's harsh desert environment, but despite their frightening appearances, they are only aggressive when disturbed or threatened. A cool mine shaft or the shady ledge of a wood shelf in an abandoned cabin in the summer heat provides a comfortable escape for desert creatures, most of which are active at night and asleep during the day. Watch where you put your hands and feet, because you may be disturbing someone's bedtime rest. Rattlesnakes enjoy coiling up in a cool place, under a rocky ledge or the shadow of old mining equipment. With one exception, all rattlesnakes possess one of two types of venom — either a hemotoxin (which acts on the blood) or a neurotoxin (which acts on the nervous system). Only the Mojave rattlesnake has both types. Rattlesnakes use their venom for two things, to kill their prey and self-defense. If you come across a rattlesnake, move away quickly, and let them go on their way undisturbed.

Scorpions nest under rocks during the day. They have terrible eyesight despite the fact that they have at least four or five eyes. The sting from a scorpion is usually no more severe than a bee sting and the pain usually goes away within a few hours. There are a few deadly species, which are characterized by a small horn-like growth under their stingers, but they are primarily found in the Sonoran Desert of southern Arizona and northern Mexico.

There are many wild and fascinating creatures in the desert that have carved an existence from the harsh and unforgiving environment. They deserve our respect, not our fear. Observe them and let them go about their business undisturbed.

HEAT-RELATED ILLNESS

FIRST AID KIT

Every car or daypack should have a basic first aid kit. Some suggested items for a compact first aid kit are: roll of one inch waterproof tape (good for wrapping on the heel or across toes to prevent blisters); moleskin; 2.25" x 3" adhesive gauze pads; Band-Aids; one or two rolls of gauze; an antibacterial ointment; potable aqua tabs or iodine crystals for emergency water purification; aspirin; antacid; mosquito repellent; sunscreen; alcohol pads or biodegradable soap; whistle; mirror; emergency blanket; spare packets of ERG; ankle brace (for sprained ankles) and a pair of tweezers (for removal of cactus spines or ticks). Needle nose pliers are excellent for removing cactus balls.

HEAT EXHAUSTION

Heat exhaustion is a serious heat-related illness which occurs when the body rate of heat gain is greater than the rate of heat loss. The best way to avoid heat exhaustion is to drink adequate water with electrolyte additive. There are a number of factors that can cause heat exhaustion. Dehydration (not drinking enough water) and physical overexertion when it's hot are the two biggest causes. Symptoms include physical weakness, dizziness, nausea, vomiting, minimal or no urination and headache. As soon as symptoms are identified, the victim should be moved out of direct sunlight. He or she should sit or lie down, preferably with feet elevated, and slowly drink a fluid, such as water, containing ERG. Movement should be limited until body fluids are fully restored.

HEAT STROKE

Heat stroke occurs when the body's internal temperature rises above 105 degrees, and can result in death if not treated immediately. Hikers who are not used to the desert's hot temperatures may suffer from "exertional" heat stroke if they prolong their hiking activity. Initial symptoms will include pale, damp, cool skin even when their internal temperature has reached dangerous levels — followed by confused, irrational, even aggressive behavior and physical collapse. During the summer, early fall and late spring, when desert temperatures inch up to the triple digits, many visitors to the desert southwest, who are not used to desert hiking, might suffer symptoms of "classic" heat stroke. Their skin will be hot and dry to touch with dangerously high internal temperature. In both cases, the goal of treatment should be to quickly reduce the body temperature. Place victim in the shade, remove or loosen tight clothing and aggressively cool the victim by pouring water over them, or swabbing them with water-soaked cloths or bandannas and fanning. If the victim is conscious, have them drink water in sips. The victim must be evacuated and hospitalized.

HYPONATREMIA

Hyponatremia or water intoxication occurs when a person drinks an excessive amount of water without replacing lost electrolytes either by not eating or not including an electrolyte replacement supplement in the water. Initial symptoms are similar to those of heat exhaustion — physical weakness, dizziness, nausea with frequent urination, which can result in seizures, collapse and unconsciousness.

HYPOTHERMIA

Hypothermia is caused by exposure to cold and moisture, and if ignored can cause death. Hypothermia occurs when the body experiences heat loss causing the body's core temperature to drop, impairing brain and muscular functions. The most common way to get hypothermia is by not dressing warmly enough to insulate the body from adverse environmental elements including, but not limited to, exposure to cold, rain, snow and wind. Initial symptoms include feeling very cold, numbness of skin, minor muscular impairment. As the body temperature drops, the muscles become increasingly uncoordinated, there is mild confusion, slowness of pace, apathy or amnesia. If not treated immediately, it can progress to unconsciousness and eventually death.

Preventing hypothermia requires warm dry clothing, food and water. Once again, drinking water and snacking on foods high in carbohydrates at frequent intervals will provide and restore energy supplies for physical activity and production of body heat. Most importantly, dress in layers. Wool and polyester are the best insulators. A layer of polypropylene long underwear, tops and bottoms, followed by wool or synthetic sweater and pants, topped off with a waterproof, breathable layer of nylon — jacket and pants which can double as rain and wind protection. The final critical item is a wool or polyester weave hat since a large percentage of heat loss occurs at the head. Include on the list, a warm pair of gloves and socks. If a person comes down with hypothermia, removing their wet clothing and warming them with another human body can be a life-saver. Climbing into a sleeping bag with them can help restore their body temperature.

In winter, Nevada highways and remote roads have claimed their share of lives during unexpected snowfalls. One couple, who went up to the mountains for a day near Lake Tahoe, were trapped on a road during a heavy snow and eventually died of exposure. No one knew where they were and they weren't found by road crews until the spring thaw. There is also the story of the young couple and their baby who tried to take a shortcut along a Nevada highway during a snowstorm and were trapped by heavy snow. The mother and baby took shelter in rocks and waited while the young husband walked along the highway. He was found days later by road crews out to plow the road. Thankfully, all survived but both parents suffered frostbite on their feet.

INDEX

IMPORTANT ADDRESSES AND PHONE NUMBERS

Bureau of Land Management,
Bishop Field Office
351 Pacu Lane, Ste. 100
Bishop, CA 93514
Phone (760)872-5000
Fax (760)872-5050
Web: www.blm.gov/ca/st/en/fo/bishop.html

Bureau of Land Management,
Las Vegas Field Office
4701 North Torrey Pines
Las Vegas, NV 89130
Phone (702)515-5000
Web: www.blm.gov/nv/st/en/fo/lvfo.html

Bureau of Land Management,
Tonopah Field Station
1553 S. Main Street
Tonopah, NV 89049-0911
Phone (775)482-7800
Fax (775)482-7810
Web: www.nv.blm.gov/bmountain/

Death Valley National Park
P.O. Box 579
Death Valley, California 92328-0579
Phone (760)786-3200
Fax (760)786-3283
Web: www.nps.gov/deva

Desert National Wildlife Range
c/o Desert Complex
HCR 38, Box 700
Las Vegas, NV 89124
Phone (702)879-6110
Web: www.fws.gov/desertcomplex/

Lake Mead National Recreation Area
601 Nevada Way
Boulder City, NV 89005
Phone (702)293-8900
Web: www.nps.gov/lame

Las Vegas Metropolitan Police Department
Search and Rescue
Call 911 for Emergencies
(Responsible for 8,000 square miles of desert)
2990 N. Rancho Dr.
Las Vegas, Nevada 89130
702-828-3567
Web: www.lvmpdsar.com/

Mojave National Preserve
Mojave National Preserve
2701 Barstow Road
Barstow, CA 92311
Phone (760)252-6100
Web: www.nps.gov/moja/

Mojave National Preserve
Kelso Depot Visitor Center
From Interstate 15, exit at Baker, California. Kelso is 35 miles south of Baker. From Interstate 40, exit on Kelbaker Road. Kelso is 22 miles north of I-40 on Kelbaker Road. Open 9-6 daily except Christmas.
Phone (760)252-6108

Red Rock Canyon
National Conservation Area
HCR 33, Box 5500
Las Vegas, NV 89124
Visitor Center: (702)515-5362

Toiyabe National Forest-
Spring Mountains National Recreation Area
4701 North Torrey Pines
Las Vegas, NV 89130
Phone (702)515-5400
Web: www.fs.fed.us/htnf

Valley of Fire State Park
P.O. Box 515
Overton, NV 89040
Phone (702)397-2088
Web: http://parks.nv.gov/vf.htm

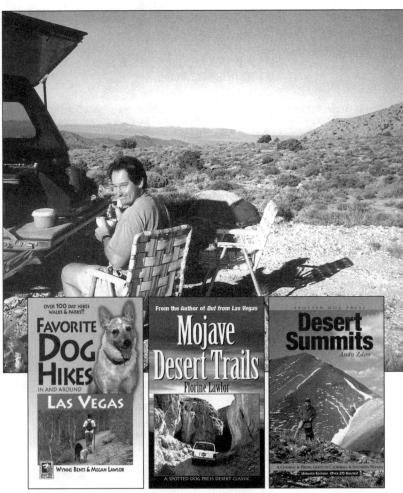

PUBLISHING DESERT BOOKS SINCE 1995

SPOTTED
DOG PRESS.